Appalachian
TRADITIONS

MOUNTAIN WAYS OF CANNING, PICKLING & DRYING

by lesa w. postell

lesa w. postell

Edited by Amy Ammons Garza

COVER ART & DESIGN BY DOREYL AMMONS CAIN

AMMONS COMMUNICATIONS, LTD.
64 WINDSONG LANE, WHITTIER, NC 28789

First Edition

*Cover illustration is of author's
maternal grandparents:
David A. and Truley McGaha Harverson*

PUBLISHED BY:
AMMONS COMMUNICATIONS, LTD.
64 WINDSONG LANE, WHITTIER, NC 28789
PHONE & FAX 1-704-631-9203

LIBRARY OF CONGRESS CATALOG CARD NO: 99-095458

ISBN: 0-9651232-7-8

Dedicated to four strong mountain women who have been instrumental in my life, giving me encouragement and being such wonderful role models.

My mom Candace, who always believes in me.

1945 —

Aunt Mae, who patiently taught me how to cook.

1907 — 1990

Grandma Truley, who introduced me to native plants and their uses.

1907 — 1993

Mama Matheson, my husband's great grandmother, who loved and accepted me from day one.

1898 — 1985

FORWARD

L ong before modern day grocery stores, America's native people, farmers, settlers, and housewives grew and gathered their own food. It was imperative to be able to store food for winter's use during a time when food became scarce. Due to necessity, food storage techniques were developed.

Appalachian Traditions—Mountain Ways Of Canning, Pickling, & Drying, is based on authentic sources, including five generations of family recipes handed down through oral tradition, and personal journals. Arranged by subject, this collection of old-time family how-to's which was once the necessity of life, still remain an ever present reality of mountain life. While learning about the book's subject matter, family stories have been inserted to create a sense of being in a time not so long ago and make the book more enjoyable. Learning old-time food preservation need not be so exhaustive, confusing, or boring. My hope is to fascinate, enlighten, and perhaps restore the interest in home food preservation and our Appalachian heritage. Some or perhaps many of the subjects may be new to you; thus instructions are presented as simply as possible and maintained in an old fashioned manner.

Some references to modern day equipment or procedures will be used occasionally to help with the time constraints placed upon modern lifestyles. You will not be encumbered with excessive equipment and materials. Each process discussed requires only creative thought and moderate expense.

Approach each procedure with the idea of doing something with nothing. If you are not satisfied with a result keep practicing or make adjustments. Remember to think safety and do not get discouraged. Once you have mastered a procedure, you will more than likely want to do more.

Whether you are learning the art of food preservation for economic help, historical value, or an enjoyable pastime, you will benefit from this volume. ❑

ABOUT THE AUTHOR

I grew up in Jackson County, nestled within the most beautiful place on earth, the Great Smoky Mountains of North Carolina. A place where simplicity is the charm of life; where hard work and sometimes a harsh environment are taken in stride.

My mother was age ninteen when she married my father, age fifty-nine. Although my father was much older than my mother, I never noticed. It was like having a daddy and a grandfather all in one. He shared with us many fascinating family stories which had been passed down through the years; thus I was born into a unique situation which allowed me a distinct taste of the past.

Daddy, Mama, my brother Allen, and I lived in a large house with Uncle Roy and Aunt Mabel; Daddy's sister, whom we called Aunt Mae for short. Growing up in the little town of Sylva had a "safe" feeling. We never locked our doors and everyone knew everyone else. The highlight of our week came when we traveled the little winding road across Balsam Mountain into Haywood county. My mother's people came from this county. Mama's family was quite large (10 sisters and brothers), so there were always lots of cousins to play with while visiting Grandpa and Grandma.

Changes taking place everyday I didn't even notice. Four-lane highways were being built in the early 1970's and an influx of people were shopping in our stores with strange accents. Tourists were a normal occurrence in the summer months, but in autumn they would leave like the leaves from the trees. Our communities had been virtually untouched before this. Watching and experiencing many changes were confusing to me. New highways replaced the old ones, shopping centers were built, and fast food restaurants emerged. The older men seen standing outside talking in front of the drug store had ceased, locking our doors became a must, and people became more interested in keeping up with the world than understanding their past.

Family systems were changing, too, due to the introduction of new ideas—families leaving the area for better jobs and the eventual deaths of our older people whom had been catalysts in keeping our hearts and minds connected to each other and the earth. Divorce became increasingly commonplace, and children were left with little understanding of their family history.

I was a fortunate child, taught to rise early in the morning. During many of those mornings, I watched the sunrise and experienced the sweet aroma of wild honeysuckle while hoeing in the garden. I learned so much about life and the connection between all of God's creation here in these mountains. I married on the crest of my sixteenth year to Kenneth Postell who, at the time, was almost eighteen years old. Our journey together is now approaching twenty years.

During the first several years of marriage, my husband and I began to understand the valuable lessons of our childhood concerning patience, hard work, and the ability to be self-sufficient. Marriage has not been easy; we learned that relationships take much work. After a year and a half, a son was born to us—we named him Bronce after his great, great grandpa Bronce Matheson. Our family members helped us greatly with child rearing and other problems we faced. Their knowledge never ceased to amaze me. The information I learned, diverse with advice unsurpassed, is part of who I am today—yet most of these mountaineer's suggestions would not have been accepted by the modern world, then or now.

In the year of 1984, after I had been married for four years and was raising a three year old child, my father died suddenly from a heart attack. He had been approaching his eightieth birthday. A few years earlier we had lost Uncle Roy, which had left a void and...now Daddy. This was very difficult for my family.

Within the next year we lost my husband's great grandma, Mama Matheson and a short time later Aunt Mae died. Grandpa Harverson had died several years earlier and was now to be joined by Grandma Truley at their eternal resting place in Maggie Valley. This was an incredible amount of loss for a young family, but we held fast to the teachings of these and other inspiring mountaineers.

I give honor to my family and ancestors by presenting this valuable, long forgotten information about canning and food preservation to you. It is my hope to preserve these methods, handed down to me concerning the art of food storage from yesteryear—to be carried on and rekindled

in the children of the future.

lesa w. postell

Associate of Applied Science, 1995 Southwestern Community College

Bachelor of Science, 1997 Western Carolina University

Phi Theta Kappa, National Honors Society Pi Gamma Mu, International Honors Society

lesa currently resides in the Greens Creek Community of Jackson County, North Carolina with her husband, Kenneth, and her son, Bronce, where they have chosen to live the lifestyle of their heritage.

Appalachian Traditions

Coming Soon!

Appalachian Traditions: Mastering Meathouse Matters

by lesa w. postell

Topics covered will include animal care, slaughter preparation, cutting tools/equipment, slaughter, post slaughter, old-fashioned processing methods and storage of meats.

Old-time processing methods covered will include—salt curing, smoking, jerkying, pickling and canning.

Appalachian Traditions: Mastering Meathouse Matters is an informative volume spotlighting by-gone methods of home meat processing from the pen to the table. In keeping with the first volume, it is my hope to present the information in simple terms, easy to learn.

This second volume will also hold family recipes that have been passed down and used for generations. Some of the recipes will include dry cures and wet cures, sausage, head cheese, pickled pigs feet, corned beef, livermush and more.

To order this second book in a series, send $15 and $3 handling charge to:

lesa w. postell
P.O. Box 887, Sylva, NC 28779

APPALACHIAN TRADITIONS

Mountain Ways of Canning, Pickling, & Drying

CONTENTS

A SEED

EARTH FROM WHICH MAN NOW TROD
WAS ONCE THE CLAY HE WAS MADE OF

A DARK, WARM BED WITH COVERS OF LEAVES
LIE STILL BENEATH FUTURE PLANTS AND TREES

THE SEED KNOWS HIS IMPORTANCE NO DOUBT
FROM THE EARTHS WOMB, ALL THINGS MUST SPROUT

THE RAIN AND SUN SHARE NO STRIFE
THEY UNDERSTAND WHAT BRINGS FORTH LIFE

THE MIGHTY OAK FEELS NO SHAME
FOR FROM HIS BRANCHES SHADE BECAME

AS THE FIELDS OF GOLD DISPLAYED OF WHEAT
GIVE UNTO MAN, GRAIN OF WHICH TO EAT

ALL GREAT AND SMALL, BELOW AND ABOVE
SHARE THE CYCLE OF LIFE, GOD'S PLAN IN LOVE

WHAT A MIRACLE NO MATTER THE SEED
WITHOUT INSPIRATION, NOTHING WOULD BE INDEED

—lesa w. postell

CHAPTER ONE

Home Food Preservation
"Putting Up Food For The Winter."

It seems the kitchen is the place where the seasons dictate the activities. Preserving the harvest is still as important to my family today as it was for my great grandparents. We can, pickle, and dry almost everything and go to the store very seldom. When you raise everything you eat it doesn't take much extra. I suppose self-sufficiency is just bred into mountain people; although some do choose to leave their roots.

Not only is it a gratifying feeling to know one can feed oneself, but if a disaster, a war, hard times, or an illness occurs; it's a secure feeling to have one's own food supply. The mountain people for many years lived in deep isolation

1

back in the hollows and coves of the Smokies and had to make do with what they had and was thankful. Unlike the people of today who grumble over temporary interruptions of conveniences; such as electrical outages.

As a child growing up in the mountains I always worked hard in the garden, and even though it was a chore, I enjoyed seeing the fruits of my labor. Hard work, determination, and faith were instilled in me which created a strong sense of responsibility, creativity, and humbleness that has helped me to develop a healthy attitude toward life, family, and uncertainty.

That is what home preservation of food is all about. Ensuring that your family members have the needed food supply to maintain their health and happiness. This is not an easy task, but well worth the time and effort expended. So I not only enjoy home food preservation, but I know that my family is living their mountain heritage to the fullest—learning, teaching, and sharing the gift of traditions of kindred and enjoying the simplicity of life.

Now you too may walk the hills with my people and experience the traditions which have been past down to ensure our survival.

Getting Started

Canning in the mountain counties of North Carolina has only been present since the mid to late 1800's. Those who had more wealth were able to obtain the new jars first. Canning (only one of the methods used to preserve food) is a method of using heat and airtight jars to preserve foods close to the condition of freshly cooked. Canning equipment can be purchased new or used. If buying new it can run into money, but when obtained used it is only a moderate expense. If you decide to buy used jars, canners, etc. make sure that the equipment is in good condition free of chips, cracks, flaking enamel, and the like.

Start collecting items in the order of priority, then you may add gadgetry later if you wish. Some items may be made yourself, improvise where possible.

Open Kettle Method

The OPEN KETTLE method is where food is cooked until done in an open kettle or pan. Then the food is packed boiling hot into jars and sealed immediately. Only pickles and jellies are canned by this method (It is not a recommended process by modern day food science). All other foods must be processed.

Hot Water Bath

Any container that has a tight fitting lid to keep steam from escaping and deep enough to allow the water level to come across the jars will serve. Place a metal rack or wooden slats in the bottom of the container to raise the jars off the bottom.   Processing time begins as soon as the water comes to a rolling boil.   Add more boiling water as needed to keep the appropriate water level (wash tubs with wooden or tin covers were used for this purpose before water bath canners were readily available).

Pressure Canner

Pressure canning is a popular modern day method, which uses steam pressure to drive out the remaining air and cooks at a higher temperature.   Place the filled jars on a rack inside the canner which contains about 2 or 3 inches of hot water and secure the lid.   Let a steady flow of steam escape for 10 minutes to exhaust any remaining air before placing the jiggler (weighted gage) on top (dial gauge models are available as well).   This method is the only recommended process in modern day food science labs for certain foods such as vegetables, non-acid foods, and meats.   References to this method of processing can be obtained by acquiring a Ball Blue Book or other modern day canning guide.

When using a pressure canner I personally prefer the model with the jiggler; it works better on my wood cookstove and I can hear any changes in the canner, rather than having to continually look at the dial gauge. Safe canning means paying careful attention to each step during the process beginning with the selection of food items, cleanliness of the kitchen, checking jars for chipped rims or cracks, having new lids ready, sterilizing of equipment to be used, and finally testing the seal before storing.

Most fruits, vegetables, and meats may be canned two ways: cold packed (raw) or hot packed (precooked). I personally use both methods, because sometimes one procedure works better for my needs than another.

Steps In Canning

1. Select good quality food, wash thoroughly in several changes of water to remove soil. Inspect for insects and debris.

2. Wash jars and other equipment well before using. Place jars and flat lids in hot water until ready to use.

3. Prepare the fruit, vegetable, or other item for canning by paring, coring, slicing, pitting, crushing, grinding, etc.

4. Choose either the cold pack (raw) or hot pack (precooked) method.

5. Make syrup ahead of time for fruits, so there is no delay in processing.

6. Precook those foods which require precooking.

7. Remove one jar at a time from the place where the jars have been held in hot water.

8. Pack the jars quickly with prepared food to the recommended head space.

9. Pour hot water or liquid over the food item up to appropriate level of head space.

10. Work out the air bubbles by running a non-metallic spatula or knife up and down the inside of jars to keep liquid above the food. Add additional liquid if needed.

11. For vegetables and meats add 1 teaspoon of canning salt to each quart and 1/2 teaspoon to each pint.

12. Wipe jar rim with a damp cloth to remove any food particles, salt, or syrup from the rim. Place the flat dome lid down onto the clean jar rim. Place the metal screw ring on the jar and tighten.

13. Process immediately, using desired canning method. Make sure that the canning method being used is followed closely. Process at the appropriate temperature for the required length of time. A canning guide has been inserted in this book to help you (see page 8 & 9), or use the time charts from the Ball Blue Book.

After Processing

1. Be careful to lift hot jars from the canner by the jar rim, not the screw band. Place hot jars to cool in a draft free area of the kitchen, so not to break the hot jars.

2. Place a thick towel or cloth down on the table to be used and place jars upright on the towel away from drafts. Keep the jars from touching each other. Place another towel on top of the jars while cooling.

3. Do not open jars or screw down loose fitting bands.

4. Allow the jars to cool. You will hear popping sounds coming from the jars as they begin to cool—this is a sign of sealing.

5. When cool you may remove the towel or cloth and check for sealing. To test the seal on jars, press the center of the lid; if lid is firmly down and does not rise back up, the jar is sealed.

6. Some jars may not have sealed for whatever reason. If the jar is not sealed use contents immediately ; or check jars for flaws and begin reprocessing.

7. Hint: wipe off the outside of jars with a damp cloth of vinegar and water solution; this will keep down outside mildew growth on jars.

8. Label the jar for content and date canned by writing on the lid with a permanent marker before storing.

9. Remove screw bands and store your canned goods in a cool, dry, dark place until used. Make sure not to knock filled jars against one another and leave a small amount of space between jars being stored.

10. When opening foods check for signs of spoilage such as: leaks, bulging lids, spurting, or off-odor. Never use or taste foods with these signs.

Guide and Timetable

ITEM	PROCEDURE	WATER BATH IN MINUTES	PRESSURE CANNER MIN. AT 5 LBS.
Apples	Hot Pack	20	10
Applesauce	Hot Pack	20	5
Berries (except strawberries)			
	Cold Pack	20	10
	Hot Pack	15	5
Cherries	Cold Pack	20	10
	Hot Pack	10	5
Grapes	Cold Pack	20	10
	Hot Pack	10	5
Peaches	Cold Pack	25	10
	Hot Pack	10	5
Pears		20	10
Plums	Cold Pack	25	10
	Hot Pack	10	5
Rhubarb	Cold Pack	20	10
	Hot Pack	10	5
Strawberries	Cold Pack	15	10
	Hot Pack	10	5
Fruit Juices	Hot Pack	15	NA
Pickles	Seal	15	NA
Jellies	Seal	5	NA

Guide and Timetable

ITEM	PROCEDURE	WATER BATH IN HOURS	PRESSURE CANNER MIN. AT 10 LBS.
Green Beans		3 hrs	25
Beets		2 1/2 hrs	35
Broccoli		2 1/2 hrs	40
Cabbage		2 1/2 hrs	40
Carrots		2 1/2 hrs	30
Corn, Creamed style (pints only)		4 hrs	85
Corn, Whole Kernel		4 hrs	85
Corn on the Cob		4 hrs	85
Greens, All Kinds		3 1/2 hrs	105
Hominy		2 hrs	45
Okra		3 hrs	40
Peas		3 1/2 hrs	45
Potatoes, New White		2 1/2 hrs	45
Potatoes, Sweet		4 hrs	120
Pumpkin		3 1/2 hrs	105
Sauerkraut		20 minutes	NA
Tomatoes		45 minutes	NA

Meats: Lamb, Beef, Veal, Pork, Bear, Venison, Groundhog			
	Cold Pack	3 1/2 hrs	90
	Hot Pack	3 1/2 hrs	90
Pork Sausage	Hot Pack/Seal	15 minutes	5
Pork Sausage/*ground meat*			
	Hot Pack only	3 1/2 hrs	90
Meats: Poultry, Chicken, Duck, Turkey, Rabbit, Squirrel			
Hot Pack or Cold Pack *with bones*		3 1/2 hrs	75
Hot Pack or Cold Pack *without bones*		3 1/2 hrs	90
Fish:			
Trout	Cold Pack	4 hrs	100
Smoked Trout	Cold Pack	4 hrs	90

A BEAN

WHAT DOES IT MEAN
TO BE A GREEN BEAN
SLIM FROM TOP TO BOTTOM
TO SNAP AND POP
AFTER THE STRING HAS DROPPED
UNLESS OF COURSE IT'S ROTTEN
A CHERISHABLE THOUGHT
TO BE "COOKED IN A POT"
-- A MEAL NOT SOON FORGOTTEN

—lesa w. postell

CHAPTER TWO

The Canhouse
*"It gives me great pride to see what I 'put up'
with my own two hands."*

Autumn, a most splendid season—when leaves are seen dancing in circular motion, showing off their array of colors. The dark, cool earth below is waiting patiently for the leaves to give way and rest upon her amber skin. This is a happy time of year, even though the work is exhausting. In autumn, children can be seen in the mountains and valleys helping their families harvest the goodness of the earth. County people call this a time of "putting up." And once the food is "put up," it is stored in the "canhouse"—a small well built structure made out of rock, wood, cement blocks, etc., usually built somewhere close to the main house. Many times the structure is built so it will go back into the mountainside.

Within a typical canhouse it is not unusual to see 300 to 800 jars filled with food. Shelves are constructed in the room to hold the filled jars. These shelves are constructed from boards set onto cement blocks, or other shelving materials at hand. Root crops such as potatoes and turnips may be stored in bins directly in the open room. Other items such as apples, pears, and pumpkins are stored in baskets or bins as well. Extremely low temperatures may require additional insulation such as straw or old blankets to cover produce. The old-time methods of putting food by bring families and friends together to share in the grandeur of the season and the goodness of home preserved meals.

If you live in an area where the temperature in fall and winter averages somewhere near freezing, then you too can have a canhouse. They are not hard to construct and can be as small or large as you desire. Many people use basements to store foods as well. Canhouses may be dug out in a bank, placed underground, or a free standing building on a northern slope, with trees to shelter from the sun. How ever you decide to construct your personal canhouse is entirely up to you.

"What Would We Do Without 'Taters.'"

GRANDMA TRULEY

Spring is a season of renewal, a time to plant the crops once again. The seed that had been saved from the previous year was brought out for planting. I still plant Hickory Cane corn because it makes good hominy and bread. Corn was definitely a staple, but so were beans and them "good ole taters."

I remember My Daddy saying, "I've eat so

many taters in my life...sometimes I don't want to see another damned ole 'tater.'" Yet, when we went to the plant the garden, guess what we planted first— "taters."

I don't know what we would do with out taters! You can cook them so many ways. You can boil, bake, mash, fry, and then there's tater cakes, hash browns, tater soup, and tater candy. Of course there were sweet taters too.

It is customary in the spring to grabble out new potatoes from the dirt underneath the plant, cooking them in fat grease. They are served with corn bread, onions, and wild greens, such as "poke sallet," topping off the meal with a big glass of fresh sweet milk or perhaps a glass of creamy buttermilk (with the fakes of golden butter still floating on top). A true mountaineer would rather have this kind of meal than a steak dinner.

Well, this was just the kind of meal my Grandma Truley intended to have one late spring day. She had been studying about such a meal and decided to go out into the garden and grabble out some new potatoes. Grandma was expecting again and she had a powerful hankering for some fresh wholesome food. She decided that she would take one of her daughters out to the garden to help her gather what was needed for the meal.

"Come on Frances, let's go and git us some taters," she called.

Frances did as her mother had said and readied herself for the task. Grandma had a big kitchen spoon which she used for the job. It was just the right size and worked really well. She used a metal bucket to put the potatoes in. It would take several potatoes to feed the family.

When they reached the garden Grandma and Aunt Frances knelt down on the ground. It was exceedingly hot and the sun shone brightly upon their thick coal-black hair. They began digging out the most beautiful potatoes, about the size of a goose egg. As Grandma dug deep into the furrow moving slowly down the row, Aunt Frances placed the potatoes into the bucket. While digging deeply into the black rich dirt, suddenly something came out of a hole reaching forward with a mighty blow. Grandma was surprised and backed up, pulling Aunt Frances with her. The beautiful dress she was wearing was covered in a greenish water. When she reached up to touch her face, she rubbed the liquid from her face. She began hollering, "Dave! Come Quick!"

Aunt Frances, terribly frightened, stood frozen. Then, realizing what had happened, cried out also for her daddy.

Grandpa came as fast as he could, getting there only a short time after hearing Grandma's distressed call. Grandpa Dave saw where the big rattler had struck and grazed her face—her head had already swollen enormous. He hurried quickly to get her to a doctor.

The doctor gave Grandma some medicine for the snake bite. She was very sick for some time. The doctor told the family to bury her brand new, store-bought dress...probably the only store-bought dress she had owned. It would have been risky to have kept the dress.

Since childhood, Grandma had carried an ankle scar left by a copperhead. Now, this strong mountain women had once again survived the encounter of a poisonous snake.

NO WARNING TODAY

UNDER THE DEEP GREEN "TATER" LEAVES
GRANDMA DUG THE DIRT AWAY
A HEAPING MOUND TO BEHOLD
DINNER BELLS WILL RING WITHOUT DELAY

PUT 'EM IN A BUCKET, FILL 'EM UP HIGH
TILL THEY ALMOST RUN OUT
KNOWING SHE WOULD FIND MORE, NO DOUBT

DIGGING INTENTLY WITH HER SILVER SPOON
KNOWING SHE HAD PLANTED
BY THE SIGNS OF THE MARCH MOON

WITHOUT A WARNING AND TO HER DISMAY
FROM OUT OF THE WARM GROUND
A SNAKE CAME HER WAY

ALL BLACK WITH DIAMONDS TO MARK
WITH A POWERFUL STRIKE
THEN SUDDENLY, ALL THINGS BECAME DARK

SHE CALLED OUT "HELP" IN DISTRESS
VENOM RAN DOWN HER CHEEK
ONTO A NEWLY BOUGHT SUNDAY DRESS

THE DR MADE READY FOR HER TO BE SEEN
PAIN AND SWELLING BEFELL
HER STOIC DEMEANOR BECAME VERY LEAN

MY DEAR OLD GRANDMOTHER
TOLD THIS STORY, TRUE
HOW WARNINGS DON'T ALWAYS
SOUND OUT LOUDLY TO YOU

—lesa w. postell

CHAPTER THREE

Putting Up Vegetables

GREEN BEANS

COLD PACK

Remove strings and break green beans into 2 inch pieces. Trim out any dark spots. Wash beans in cold water. Pack beans into jars, leaving 1 inch head space. Place 1 tsp. of salt into each quart jar. Pour hot water over beans, leaving 1 inch of head space. Remove air bubbles. Wipe jar rims with a clean, damp cloth. Adjust lids and process.

HOT PACK

Remove strings and break green beans into 2 inch pieces. Trim out any dark spots. Wash beans in cold water. Put beans in a large kettle and boil 5 minutes. Ladle beans into hot jars, leaving 1 inch head space. Place 1 tsp. of salt into each quart jar. Pour hot water over beans, leaving 1 inch of head space. Remove air bubbles. Wipe jar rims with a clean, damp cloth. Adjust lids and process.

BEETS

HOT PACK

Wash beets well in cold water. Trim off leafy tops, leaving about 1 1/2 inch of the stem. Bring a large kettle of water to boil, place beets into the water and cook until tender. Plunge beets into cold water, peel and trim ends if necessary. Leave the beets whole or slice. Ladle beets into hot jars, leaving 1 inch head space. Place 1 tsp. of salt into each quart jar. Pour hot water over beets, leaving 1 inch of head space. Remove air bubbles. Wipe jar rims with a clean, damp cloth. Adjust lids and process.

BROCCOLI

COLD PACK

Wash well in cold water. Remove large leaves. Split large stalks. Pack broccoli into jars, leaving 1 inch head space (do not precook). Place 1 tsp. of salt into each quart jar. Pour hot water over broccoli, leaving 1 inch of head space. Remove air bubbles. Wipe jar rims with a clean, damp cloth. Adjust lids and process.

CABBAGE

HOT PACK

Wash, remove outside leaves. Quarter cabbage head, remove stalk. Cut into desired size pieces and precook for 5 minutes. Pack cabbage into jars, leaving 1 inch head space. Place 1 tsp. of salt into each quart jar. Pour hot water over cabbage, leaving 1 inch of head space. Remove air bubbles. Wipe jar rims with a clean, damp cloth. Adjust lids and process.

CARROTS

COLD PACK

Wash well, scrape, or peel to remove skins. Slice or leave whole. Pack carrots into jars, leaving 1 inch head space. Place 1 tsp. of salt into each quart jar. Pour hot water over carrots, leaving 1 inch of head space. Remove air bubbles. Wipe jar rims with a clean, damp cloth. Adjust lids and process.

HOT PACK

Wash well, scrape, or peel to remove skins. Slice or leave whole. Precook for 5 minutes. Ladle carrots into hot jars, leaving 1 inch head space. Place 1 tsp. of salt into each quart jar. Pour hot water over carrots, leaving 1 inch of head space. Remove air bubbles. Wipe jar rims with a clean, damp cloth. Adjust lids and process.

CREAM STYLE CORN

9 cups of cut off corn
4 cups of water
1 cup of sugar
2 1/2 tsp. salt

COLD PACK
Pick corn in the milk stage. Husk, silk, and wash well. Cut corn off the cob in two rounds (tip ends first time around, scrape cob with back of knife the second time around). Place corn into a large pot and mix in other ingredients. Pack cold corn loosely into hot pint jars, leaving 1 inch head space. Remove air bubbles. Wipe jar rims with a clean, damp cloth. Adjust lids and process.

HOT PACK
Pick corn in the milk stage. Husk, silk, and wash well. Cut corn off the cob in two rounds (tip ends first time around, scrape cob with back of knife the second time around). Place corn into a large pot and mix in other ingredients. Bring to a boil for 5 minutes. Ladle corn into hot pint jars, leaving 1 inch head space. Remove air bubbles. Wipe jar rims with a clean, damp cloth. Adjust lids and process.

WHOLE KERNEL CORN

COLD PACK
Pick corn in the milk stage. Husk, silk, and

wash well. Cut corn off the cob whole. DO NOT SCRAPE. Pack corn loosely into hot jars, leaving 1 inch head space. Remove air bubbles. Wipe jar rims with a clean, damp cloth. Adjust lids and process.

HOT PACK

Pick corn in the milk stage. Husk, silk, and wash well. Cut corn off the cob whole. DO NOT SCRAPE. Put corn into a large pot, bring to a boil for 5 minutes. Ladle whole kernel corn into hot jars, leaving 1 inch head space. Remove air bubbles. Wipe jar rims with a clean, damp cloth. Adjust lids and process.

GREENS

Greens include: spinach, kale, mustard, turnip, or wild greens such as poke and dandelion.

HOT PACK

Wash greens well in several changes of salty water. Clean greens of soil, insects, and debris. Put a small amount of water in a large pot. Put the washed greens into the pot and cut an "x" through greens several times before cooking. Bring greens to a boil, cover and steam until wilted. Ladle greens into hot jars, leaving 1 inch head space. Place 1 tsp. of salt into each quart jar. Pour hot water over greens, leaving 1 inch of head space. Remove air bubbles. Wipe jar rims with a clean, damp cloth. Adjust lids and process.

HOMINY

HOT PACK

Put hominy in a large kettle and preheat until boiling. Ladle hominy into hot jars, leaving 1 inch head space. Place 1 tsp. of salt into each quart jar. Pour hot water over hominy, leaving 1 inch of head space. Remove air bubbles. Wipe jar rims with a clean, damp cloth. Adjust lids and process.

OKRA

HOT PACK

Gather young tender pods, wash well and remove stem end. If okra is to be used in soup, it needs to be sliced; otherwise can okra whole. Boil okra in water for 3 minutes. Ladle okra into hot jars, leaving 1 inch head space. Place 1 tsp. of salt into each quart jar. Pour hot water over okra, leaving 1 inch of head space. Remove air bubbles. Wipe jar rims with a clean, damp cloth. Adjust lids and process.

PEAS
Includes: blackeye and field peas.

HOT PACK

Pick young tender, fresh garden peas. Shell, wash, and put into a large pot containing water. Precook 5 minutes in boiling water. Pack peas loosely into hot jars, leaving 1 inch head space. Place 1 tsp. of salt into each quart jar. Pour hot water over okra, leaving 1 inch of head space. Remove air bubbles. Wipe jar rims with a clean, damp cloth. Adjust lids and process.

POTATOES

HOT PACK
Use small potatoes 2 inches or so across. Wash and peel. Put potatoes in a pot of water and bring to a boil for 10 minutes. Pack potatoes into hot jars, leaving 1 inch head space. Place 1 tsp. of salt into each quart jar. Pour hot water over potatoes, leaving 1 inch of head space. Remove air bubbles. Wipe jar rims with a clean, damp cloth. Adjust lids and process.

PUMPKIN

HOT PACK
Wash pumpkin well. Cut in half and remove seeds (save seeds to roast for a snack). Place pumpkin halves in a large pan, and bake in a moderate oven 325 degrees. After pumpkin is done scoop out the meat, thus leaving the shell behind. Put the pumpkin through a food mill if needed. Pack loosely in hot jars, leaving 1 inch head space. Remove air bubbles. Wipe jar rims with a clean, damp cloth. Adjust lids and process.

TURNIPS

HOT PACK
Wash thoroughly. Peel, and slice turnips. Boil 5 minutes. Pack turnips into hot jars, leaving 1 inch of head space. Place 1 tsp. of salt into each quart jar. Pour hot water over turnips, leaving 1 inch of head space. Remove air bubbles. Wipe jar rims with a clean, damp cloth. Adjust lids and process.

SUMMER SQUASH

Wash squash, do not pare. Cut into rounds 1/4 inch thick. Pack squash into jars, leaving 1 inch head space. Place 1 tsp. of salt into each quart jar. Pour hot water over squash, leaving 1 inch of head space. Remove air bubbles. Wipe jar rims with a clean, damp cloth. Adjust lids and process.

SWEET POTATOES

Wash sweet potatoes to remove soil and debris. Boil or steam for 20 minutes. Remove peelings. Pack sweet potatoes into jars, leaving 1 inch head space. Remove air bubbles. Wipe jar rims with a clean, damp cloth. Adjust lids and process.

TOMATOES

Wash ripe tomatoes in cold water. Trim

ends of tomatoes and remove blemishes. Put tomatoes in a wire basket and dip into boiling water for 1 minute. Plunge tomatoes into cold water. Peel, core, and half or leave whole. Pack tomatoes into jars, leaving 1 inch head space. Place 1 tsp. of salt and 1 Tbsp. lemon juice into each quart jar. Pour hot water over tomatoes, leaving 1 inch of head space. Remove air bubbles. Wipe jar rims with a clean, damp cloth. Adjust lids and process.

VEGETABLE SOUP

Water	Tomatoes	Okra
Corn	Celery	Carrots
Green beans	Onions	Potatoes

End of the season soup is a mixture of vegetables that is canned so that there is no waste. Whatever is left in the garden can go into the "soup mix" without worries of exact measurements of each item. Wash and prepare each item for cooking. Put cut up vegetables into a large pot and add enough water to make a good broth. Boil 5 minutes. Ladle soup into hot jars, leaving 1 inch head space. Place 1 tsp. of salt into each quart jar. Remove air bubbles. Wipe jar rims with a clean, damp cloth. Adjust lids and process. The vegetable that takes the longest processing time is; the processing time to be used. (If meat is to be used, process the time used for meat.)

APPLE DAY

WHEN WE'D VISIT UNCLE FRANK
HE ALWAYS HAD TO SAY
TAKE AN APPLE FOR YOURSELF
MOST ANY TIME OF DAY

AND WHEN YOU'D HAD QUITE ENOUGH
HE'D CALL YOU BACK HIS WAY
TAKE AN APPLE FOR YOURSELF
FOR LATER IN THE DAY

FRIENDS AND STRANGERS THEY IMPART
YOU DON'T HAVE TO PAY
TAKE AN APPLE FOR YOURSELF
TO EAT ALONG THE WAY

HE SITS IN HEAVEN DON'T YOU SEE
AND WHERE MAY HE BE
BESIDE THE RIVER CRYSTAL CLEAR
BENEATH AN APPLE TREE

your niece,
lesa w. postell

"Daddy always made sure we got some peaches to put up."

My dad, Hubert

CHAPTER FOUR

Fruits and Sweet Additions

CANNING FRUITS

Select firm, fresh fruit for canning. Over ripe fruit will float in jars once canned. If fruit must be held over to the next day, store in a cool place such as a refrigerator. To prevent darkening of the fruit while waiting to be canned, a pretreatment of lemon juice, salt, or a salt and vinegar solution is used. Fruits are packed, leaving 1/2 head space. Hot syrups or water are poured over fruit in jars, leaving 1/2 inch head space. Wipe the jar rims clean with a damp cloth. Adjust lids and process.

PRETREATMENT SOLUTIONS

Lemon solution
1 cup lemon juice to 1 gallon of water.

Salt solution
3 Tbsp. salt to 1 gallon of water.

Salt and vinegar solution
2 Tbsp. salt and 2 Tbsp. vinegar into 1 gallon of water.

A pretreatment solution of either lemon, salt, or a salt and vinegar solution is set aside to place the fruit into. Once the pieces have been peeled and seed removed, the pieces are cut in desired sizes and placed into the solution. When ready to can, remove fruit from the solution and rinse with cold water. The same solution may be reused. The solution keeps the fruit from turning dark.

HOW TO MAKE SYRUP WITH SUGAR

	YIELDS
Light syrup	
2 cups sugar to 1 quart water	5 cups
Medium syrup	
3 cups sugar to 1 quart water	5 1/2 cups
Heavy syrup	
5 cups sugar to 1 quart water	6 1/2 cups

Place sugar and water into a large pot. Bring syrup to a full boil. Pour over fruit while hot, leaving 1/2 inch head space.

CANNING FRUIT WITH HONEY OR CORN SYRUP

	YIELDS
Light syrup	
1 quart water to 1 1/2 cups honey or corn syrup	5 cups
Medium syrup	
1 quart water to 2 cups honey or corn syrup	5 1/2 cups
Heavy syrup	
1 quart water to 4 cups honey or corn syrup	6 cups

Place sugar and water into a large pot. Bring syrup to a full boil. Pour hot syrup over fruit, leaving 1/2 inch head space.

CANNING FRUIT WITHOUT SUGAR

Fruits may be canned without the use of sugar. Sugar is used to sweeten the foods, so sweeten according to your taste. Precooking the fruit will allow the fruit to release some of the juice and less sugar will be needed. When canning fruits without sugar, fill the jars to within 1/2 inch of the top with water or fruit juice. Adjust lids and process.

APPLES FOR PIES

COLD PACK
Select ripe apples wash, pare, and core. Cut the apples into quarters. Drop peeled fruit into pretreatment solution for a few minutes. Rinse fruit well in cold water. Fill the jars with fruit, leaving 1/2 inch head space. Fill the jars with hot syrup. Remove air bubbles. Wipe jar rims with a clean, damp cloth to remove any syrup or fruit. Adjust lids and process.

BAKED APPLES

HOT PACK
Select sound apples. Wash, core, and place apples in a pan with a little water in the bottom. Put the cores and peelings in the pan with water and bake. Bake apples until done, but not over cooked. When done drain off liquid from the pan and add 1 cup sugar to every cup of liquid. Pack apples into quart jars, pour liq-

uid into jars, leaving 1/2 inch head space. Remove air bubbles. Wipe jar rims with a clean, damp cloth. Adjust lids and process.

APPLE SAUCE

HOT PACK
Select sound apples. Wash, peel, core, and remove blemishes from apples. Quarter apples into a large kettle. Add a small amount of water and cook until soft. Press apples through a food mill. Sweeten apple sauce to taste. Reheat apple sauce to a boil. Ladle hot apple sauce into hot jars, leaving 1/2 inch head space. Remove air bubbles. Wipe jars rims with a clean, damp cloth. Adjust lids and seal.

ALL BERRIES

Berries include: Blackberries, blueberries, elder-berries, gooseberries, and strawberries.

COLD PACK
Wash berries in cold water. Fill jars with berries, leaving 1/2 inch head space. Pour hot syrup over berries, leaving 1/2 inch head space. Remove air bubbles. Wipe jar rims with a clean, damp cloth. Adjust lids and process.

HOT PACK
Wash berries in cold water. Put berries into a large pot; add 1/2 cup sugar to each quart of berries. Let the berries stand for 2 hours.

Cook until sugar dissolves and berries are hot through. Pour hot into jars, leaving 1/2 inch head space. Cover berries with boiling water, leaving 1/2 inch head space. Remove air bubbles. Wipe jar rims with a clean, damp cloth. Adjust lids and seal.

CHERRIES

COLD PACK

Wash, pit, and stem cherries. Fill jars with cherries, leaving 1/2 inch head space. Cover cherries with hot syrup, leaving 1/2 inch head space. Remove air bubbles. Wipe jar rims with a clean, damp cloth. Adjust lids and process.

HOT PACK

Wash, pit, and stem cherries. Put cherries into a large pot; add 1/2 cup sugar to each quart of cherries. Heat slowly until cherries are hot through. Pour hot cherries into jars, leaving 1/2 inch head space. Cover cherries with boiling water, leaving 1/2 inch head space. Remove air bubbles. Wipe jar rims with a clean, damp cloth. Adjust lids and seal.

PEACHES

COLD PACK

Wash peaches in cold water. Put peaches into a wire basket and plunge into pot of boiling water for 1 minute to loosen skins. Dip into cold water, and remove the skins. Cut peaches into halves and remove seed. Put peaches into pretreatment solution for a few minutes. Rinse fruit. Fill jars with peach halves, placing center down, leaving 1/2 inch head space. Cover peaches with hot syrup, leaving 1/2 inch head space. Remove air bubbles. Wipe jar rims with a clean, damp cloth. Adjust lids and process.

HOT PACK

Wash peaches in cold water. Put peaches into a wire basket and plunge into pot of boiling water for 1 minute to loosen skins. Dip into cold water, and remove the skins. Cut peaches into halves and remove seed. Put peaches into pretreatment solution for a few minutes. Rinse fruit. Put peaches into a large kettle and cook a few at a time in syrup until hot through. Fill jars with peach halves and syrup, leaving 1/2 inch head space. Cover peaches with hot syrup, leaving 1/2 inch head space. Remove air bubbles. Wipe jar rims with a clean, damp cloth. Adjust lids and process.

PEARS

HOT PACK

Wash pears. Cut into halves or quarters, peel and core. Drop halves or quarters into pretreatment solution. Rinse and drain. Cook pears in hot syrup for 5 minutes. Fill jars with pear pieces and syrup, leaving 1/2 inch head space. Cover pears with hot syrup or water, leaving 1/2 inch head space. Remove air bubbles. Wipe jar rims with a clean, damp cloth. Adjust lids and process.

PLUMS

COLD PACK

Wash plums and prick the skin with a needle to prevent bursting. Pack plums into clean jars, leaving 1/2 inch head space. Pour hot syrup over plums, leaving 1/2 inch head space. Remove air bubbles. Wipe jars rims with a clean, damp cloth. Adjust lids and process.

HOT PACK

Wash plums and prick the skin with a needle to prevent bursting. Boil 15 minutes in syrup. Fill jars with plums and syrup, leaving 1/2 inch head space. Remove air bubbles. Wipe jar rims with a clean, damp cloth. Adjust lids and seal.

QUINCES

HOT PACK

Wash ripe quinces. Wipe off the fuzz, peel, and cut. Put quinces in a large pot with syrup and boil until soft. Fill jars will quinces and syrup, leaving 1/2 inch head space. Remove air bubbles. Wipe jar rims with a clean, damp cloth. Adjust lids and seal.

RHUBARB

HOT PACK
Wash and cut rhubarb into convenient lengths (about 1 inch) without removing the skin. Put rhubarb pieces in a pot with syrup and cook until tender. Fill jars with hot rhubarb and syrup, leaving 1/2 inch head space. Remove air bubbles. Wipe jar rims with a clean, damp cloth. Adjust lids and seal.

STRAWBERRIES

1 cup sugar
2 pounds strawberries
1/2 cup strawberry juice

COLD PACK
Boil sugar and juice obtained from crushing some of the overripe berries. Cool, then add whole strawberries. Allow to boil 3 minutes. Remove from heat, cover and allow to cool 4 hours or overnight. Next day pack into jars, leaving 1/2 inch head space. Remove air bubbles. Wipe jar rim with a clean, damp cloth. Adjust lids and process. Note: by packing strawberries this way, the berries will not float.

*"Aunt Mae used to
fascinate me
how she'd
make that jelly."*

Aunt Mae, holding my brother Allen.

AUNT MAE

A big, white two story house sheltered us throughout the seasons for many years. As a small child I realized that the seasons change four times in a year and this cycle repeated itself indefinitely. The seasons seemed to travel slowly in those days. To pass the time I would sit on the porch or in my swing and watch the wondrous world around me. Already knowing God, in my childlike way, I would sing

37

and talk to God all the time. I never got an answer, but somehow I knew He could hear me and was pleased with me. In late summer I remember lying in my bed listening to the night sounds of katydids and crickets chirping in a natural symphony of notes.

In winter the mountains and valleys became a winter-wonderland as the white glistening snow blanketed the area.

Spring brought forth soothing rain and arching rainbows, followed by wildflowers of every color, size, and shape. They seemed so numerous there could not possibly have been a name for each individual species.

By summer the mountains flourished with lush vegetation, clothed with the bounty of creation. Not only did summer bring forth enchanting greenery, but also wild berries such as strawberries, raspberries, and blackberries. These berries were canned, dried, made into wine, and of course jelly.

When I think of blackberries I am reminded of my Aunt Mae. She was much more like a grandma to me than an aunt. Her friendly face always seemed to bear a smile. It was obvious by her plump figure that the kitchen was her favorite place to be. Aunt Mae always wore an apron neatly tied around her, so not to dirty her dress. Most of the time her silver hair was covered in a web of black netting. Blackberry picking time was the only time of year I ever saw my Aunt Mae wearing a pair of paints.

Aunt Mae would borrow a pair of Uncle

Roy's pants to wear while she was in the blackberry patch. I would intently watch Aunt Mae
get ready to pick berries. After she had dressed
in Uncle Roy's Breeches and a long sleeve shirt
she would, ever so neatly, tie her wavy hair up
in a kerchief. Sitting in a strait chair she would
pull on socks and old shoes. She had already
gathered her berry picking buckets and containers the night before; they sat ready to collect the fruit.

Before leaving out, she and Uncle Roy would
tie rags dipped in kerosene oil around their
ankles to keep away the chiggers and ticks. I
remember being very young standing at the
downstairs window crying to go, but I was too
small. I watched through tears, as Aunt Mae
and Uncle Roy left walking down the rock walk-
way and onto the little plank board that crossed
the creek, until far out of sight. Upon their
return I would be so excited to see all those
buckets and washpans full of beautiful blackberries. The fruit looked so much like that of
crown jewels, I wanted to touch them.

It didn't take long for Aunt Mae and Uncle
Roy to shuck off their clothes and re-dress to
begin the chore of washing berries. Washing
the berries took time and included looking
through the fruit for bugs and debris. Then
canning the berries began.

As the berries were canned, the remaining
berries were kept in a cool place until they
could be worked up.

Jelly making came next—Aunt Mae fascinated me how she'd make that jelly. She would let me help, after I had washed my hands. As I ran to the kitchen I would feel excitement flooding my body. I couldn't be still, continually pacing around the room asking questions about our project. She would take me to a small, brown metal stool that sat in a corner. Hopping onto the stool, my feet would dangle below me. I was only five and my feet could not reach the foot rest. The tall side table allowed me a place where I could mash the berries up real good with a potato masher. Aunt Mae then took over, preparing the berry juice and straining it thoroughly. As she added the pectin and sugar, I would watch carefully. The juice would soon began to boil steadily. I knew the juice was very hot, seeing the steam rise up and dissipate into the room.

Soon she'd begin to test the thickening of the jelly. Aunt Mae did this by dipping a large spoon into the boiling mixture and dropping it back into the pot. When it was done, the spoon would hold two drops which would join in the middle to leave the spoon in one sheet.

The sweet smell of jelly was tantalizing and I couldn't wait to have a taste. The finishing touches to the jelly were to fill jars nearly full and apply several applications of paraffin onto the jelly to seal, followed by a lid and ring. Later that very day we enjoyed biscuits and jelly served with our meal.

CHAPTER FIVE

Homemade Jellies, Preserves & Butters

• MAKING JELLIES •

Preparing Fruit and Extracting Juice

To make successful jelly 1/4 of the fruit or wild berries need to be slightly under ripe. Wash fruit carefully in cold water, removing stems, and debris. Place prepared fruit in a large kettle. Chop, crush, or quarter fruits as necessary. Add just enough water to barely cover. Simmer the fruit in a covered kettle; do not boil. Cook slowly until the fruit is very soft, about 10 minutes. Strain juice by placing a clean four sack, clean white cloth, jelly bag, or double thickness of cheese cloth onto a strainer, catching the juice in a large container below.

41

DO NOT SQUEEZE the jelly bag. Simply let it run into the container freely. The jelly made from this juice will be clear. The pulp may be used to make fruit butter or jam.

Pectin, Acid and Sugar

Three items are essential to make jelly: pectin, acid, and sugar. Pectin is found more readily in slightly under ripe fruits than fully ripe fruits. Pectin is found in the more acidic (sour) fruits except strawberries, although acidic, strawberries contain very little pectin. Good jelly can be made with confidence from fruits containing only traces of pectin by mixing with pectin rich juices. Sugar is used to preserve, sweeten, and causes the juice to congeal. So in short, the acid in fruit helps to release the pectin, which works with the sugar to form a gel, there-by preserving a sweet item called jelly.

To Test Juice for Acid

To test juice for acid is simple, taste juice for tartness. If the juice does not seem tart, lemon juice or vinegar may be added to help release pectin.

To Test Juice for Pectin

Testing the pectin content determines if enough pectin is in the juice to make jelly and indicates the amount of sugar to be used. Several methods are used to determine pectin content.

METHOD 1
   Combine 1 Tbsp. cooked fruit juice, 1 tsp. sugar and 1/2 tsp. Epsom salts. Stir until salts dissolve. Let stand about 20 minutes.

METHOD 2
   Mix 1 tsp. cooked juice and 1 tsp. grain alcohol, stir slowly.

   a. Pectin rich content- will form a large
      bulky gel like mass.
   b. Moderate pectin content- will form a few
      pieces of gel like material.
   c. Poor pectin content- will form small flaky
      pieces of gel like particles.

Making Jelly Without Using Pectin

   The amount of sugar used is determined by the pectin content. The more pectin, the more sugar used. Use the formula below:

   a. Pectin rich- 1 cup of juice to 3/4 cups
      sugar.
   b. Moderate pectin- 1 cup juice to 2/3 cup
      sugar.
   c. Poor pectin- 1 cup of juice to 1/2 cup
      sugar.

Measure juice to be used in small quantities, not more than 6 or 8 cups at one time. Measure juice, put into a pot, and heat rapidly to a steady boil. Add sugar, stir well until it is dissolved. Continue to boil until jelly test is successful.

Making Jelly With Honey or Corn Syrup

Use 1 cup of honey or corn syrup for every cup of sugar called for.

Making Jelly With Added Pectin

APPLE PECTIN

2 pounds of peelings and cores.
4 cups of water
Juice of 1 lemon

Place peelings, cores, water, and juice of 1 lemon in a pot, boil for 40 minutes. Press the juice through a clean cloth bag, then strain the juice through a jelly bag, without pressing. Put strained juice into a clean pot and boil juice rapidly for 15 minutes. Pour juice into jars, leaving 1/2 inch head space. Adjust lids and seal.

To use with poor pectin juices to make jelly. Those fruits include, but are not limited to: peach, strawberry, and cherry.

Add 1 cup apple pectin to each cup of fruit juice, or use 3/4 cups sugar to 1 cup of combined fruit juice or test for pectin content.

THE JELLY TEST

Dip a spoon into the boiling liquid. Pour the liquid from the spoon. Jelly point has been reached when the drops of liquid run together and drop off the spoon in a sheet. When the jelly point has been reached remove from the heat. Skim the foam of the top. Begin to ladle jelly into dry jars. fill to within 1/4 inch of the top. Wipe the glass rims with a clean, damp cloth to remove any jelly residue.

SEALING WITH PARAFFIN

Melt paraffin in a pan over low heat until it is hot. Pour a thin layer of hot paraffin over the jelly. Roll the glass around to evenly cover the entire surface. Cool. Apply a second layer of hot paraffin to ensure a good seal. A lid may be placed on the jelly glass if desired. Label and store in a cool place. Or Adjust lids and seal by hot water bath method for 5 minutes.

APPLE JELLY

Place apple peelings into a pot with enough water to cover. Cook until peelings are soft. Strain juice through cloth bag twice. Add 3/4 cup of sugar to every cup of juice. Boil rapidly until jelly stage is reached. Ladle into jars, leaving 1/4 inch head space. Seal with paraffin or adjust lids and seal.

BLACKBERRY JELLY

Wash blackberries in cold water. Crush berries and put into a pot with a small amount of water. Boil for 15 minutes. Press though a jelly bag and strain. Measure juice and heat to boiling. For each cup of juice add 3/4 cup sugar. Boil until jelly stage is reached. Ladle into jars, leaving 1/4 inch head space. Seal with paraffin or adjust lids and seal.

CORN COB JELLY

12 medium red corn cobs
2 quarts water
3 cups apple pectin
3 cups sugar

Wash corn cobs. Cut corn cobs into quarters or beat until flattened. Put them into a pot containing 2 quarts of water. Bring to a boil. Lower heat and let boil for about 40 to 45 minutes.

Strain through a jelly bag or cheese cloth. Put 3 cups of corn cob juice in a pot and mix in the apple pectin. Bring to a boil. Add 3 cups of sugar. Boil until jelly point is reached. Ladle into jars, leaving 1/4 inch head space.

GOOSEBERRY JELLY

3 pounds gooseberries
Sugar

Wash gooseberries. Remove the stems and blossom ends. Cover with water and cook slowly until tender. Drain through a jelly bag or piece of doubled cheese cloth. Combine sugar, and juice in equal proportions. Boil rapidly until jelly point is reached. Ladle into jars, leaving 1/4 inch head space. Seal with paraffin or adjust lids and seal.

GRAPE JELLY

Wash grapes, drain off water, and put on to boil. Boil until tender. Strain through a piece of cheese cloth or a jelly bag. To 1 cup of juice add 1 cup of sugar. Bring mixture to boiling point, remove from heat. Ladle into jars, leaving 1/4 inch head space. Seal with paraffin or adjust lids and seal.

MINT JELLY

1 cup mint leaves
1 1/2 cups boiling water
1/2 cup apple juice

Pour boiling water over mint leaves. Steep for 30 minutes. Press juice from the leaves. Combine apple juice, sugar, and 2 Tbsp. mint tea in a pot. Boil rapidly till jelly stage is reached. Ladle into jars, leaving 1/4 inch head space. Seal with paraffin or adjust lids and seal.

QUINCE JELLY

Cut quinces in small pieces, cover with water and cook until tender. Strain juice through a jelly bag or a clean white cloth. Measure juice and return to pot. Bring juice to a boil and add 1 cup of sugar to every cup of juice. Boil rapidly until jelly stage is reached. Ladle into jars, leaving 1/4 inch head space. Seal with paraffin or adjust lids and seal.

WILD PLUM JELLY

Wash wild plums. Cover with water and cook until tender. Press juice through a jelly bag or piece of clean white cloth. Strain juice and measure. Place juice into a pot and bring to a boil. Add 1 cup of sugar for every cup of plum juice. Boil rapidly until jelly stage is reached. Ladle into jars, leaving 1/4 inch head space. Seal with paraffin or adjust lids and seal.

WILD RASPBERRY JELLY

3 cups raspberry juice
3 cups sugar

Wash raspberries. Place in a pot with enough water to cover. Cook raspberries until soft. Press through a jelly bag or piece of doubled cheese cloth. Measure 3 cups of juice into pot. Bring juice to a boil and add 3 cups of sugar. Boil rapidly until jelly stage is reached. Ladle into jars, leaving 1/4 inch head space. Seal with paraffin or adjust lids and seal.

• MAKING PRESERVES •

Preserves are made from various fruits and berries which are sliced, chopped, or left whole. To seal follow same directions as for jelly.

WILD BERRY PRESERVES

5 pounds of wild berries
3 pounds of sugar

Wash the berries in cold water to remove soil and debris. Put water and berries into a large kettle and cook slowly until the juice is extracted. Add sugar and boil for 20 minutes. Ladle into jars, leaving 1/4 inch head space. Adjust lids and seal.

CRAB APPLE PRESERVES

Wash ripe crab apples and remove blossom ends. Leave the stems on and do not peel. Make a syrup of 6 cups sugar and 3 cups water by boiling for 5 to 10 minutes. Put the crab apples into boiling syrup and cook until done. Ladle into jars, leaving 1/4 inch head space. Adjust lids and seal.

PEACH PRESERVES

3 cups of peaches
1/4 cup water
2 cups sugar

Peel peaches, remove seeds, and slice. Cook sliced peaches in water for 5 minutes until tender. Add sugar and cook peaches until most of the water is removed, stirring often. Cook until thick. Ladle into jars, leaving 1/4 inch head space. Seal with paraffin or adjust lids and seal.

RASPBERRY, STRAWBERRY, AND CHERRY PRESERVES

2 1/2 pints of raspberries
2 pints strawberries
1 pound cherries
Equal amount of sugar by weight of fruit.

Combine all of the ingredients and boil 25 minutes. Add 1/2 cup lemon juice and boil 3 more minutes. Remove from heat and cool. When cool pour into jars, leaving 1/4 inch head space. Seal with paraffin or adjust lids and seal.

SUNSHINE STRAWBERRY PRESERVES

8 cups strawberries
9 cups sugar
Juice of 1 lemon

Cap strawberries and wash carefully. Put strawberries into a kettle, alternating layers with sugar. Add lemon juice and heat to boiling. Boil for 10 minutes. Ladle into jars, leaving 1/4 inch head space. Set in the sun for 3 days. Seal with paraffin. (While in the sun place a piece of glass over the preserves.)

• FRUIT BUTTERS •

Butters are made of fruit which have been cooked slowly until tender and thick in just enough liquid to keep fruit from sticking. The cooked fruit is then put through a food mill. The thick fruit is then combined with sugar to sweeten. Fruit butters may be covered in paraffin like jelly and stored or lids and rings can be applied and sealed.

APPLE BUTTER

4 gallons prepared apples
1 gallon sweet cider
4 pints of sugar
1 tsp. allspice
1 tsp. cinnamon

Peel, core, and slice apples. Bring sweet cider to a boil until it is reduced by half. Add apples to boiling cider. Cook slowly, stirring often so not to scorch. When it begins to thicken add sugar and spices. Cook to desired thickness. Ladle into jars, leaving 1/4 inch head space. Adjust lids and seal.

APPLE SAUCE BUTTER

12 cups apple sauce   1 tsp. cloves
9 cups sugar   1 tsp. allspice
2 tsp. cinnamon

Pour prepared apple sauce into large pot with sugar and spices. Bring to a boil for 20 minutes or until apple butter is desired thickness. Remove from heat. Ladle apple sauce into jars, leaving 1/4 inch head space. Adjust lids and seal.

GRAPE BUTTER

Press cooked grapes through a food mill to remove seeds and skins. Measure grape pulp, add one half as much sugar. Cook until thick, stirring often. Ladle into jars, leaving 1/4 inch head space. Adjust lids and seal.

PEACH BUTTER

Scald peaches in boiling water and plunge into cold water; peel and remove seeds. Cook to a pulp in a pot containing just enough water to prevent sticking. To each cup of pulp add one half as much sugar. Cook until thick, stirring often. Ladle into jars, leaving 1/4 inch head space. Adjust lids and seal.

PEAR BUTTER

Wash pears. Do not peel. Slice. Add enough water to prevent from sticking. Cook until soft. Press cooked pears through a food mill. To each cup of pulp, add 1/2 cup sugar. Cook until thick, stirring often. Ladle into jars, leaving 1/4 inch head space. Adjust lids and seal.

PLUM BUTTER

Use the same recipe as for pear butter.

TOMATO BUTTER

4 quarts stewed tomatoes
7 cups light brown sugar
1 Tbsp. ground cloves
1 Tbsp. cinnamon
1 tsp. allspice

Put all the above ingredients into a kettle and cook slowly until thick. Ladle into jars leaving 1/4 inch head space. Adjust lids and seal.

MAMA MATHESON

*"I've won so many blue ribbons with Hot Tom,
I just quit entering it."*

Bertha Waldroop Matheson, my husband's great grandmother, was known as Mama, or Mama Matheson to most people. She was a kind, yet spirited woman who lived in the Nantahala mountain region of Western North Carolina. A petite little women, Mama weighed no more that 98 pounds soaking wet. But now don't think she couldn't handle things. She was tougher than a pine knot and twice as gritty. She had strong determination and wouldn't take "I can't" for an answer.

Mama was forever making things, whether it be clothes, pillow tops, or canning. She invented a relish many years ago that she called "Hot Tom." My husband remembers when he was a little boy how he helped in the yearly tradition of making Mama's secret relish—a recipe that she held dear to her heart. Everyone around loved her relish and there's no telling how many jars of relish that she gave away.

Mama Matheson gave me her favorite "Hot Tom" recipe when my husband and I married. Our family makes her relish yearly and I have entered Mama's relish in several fairs and never have come away without less than a blue ribbon. In fact, I've won so many ribbons with it, that I've just quit entering the contests.

I remember one fall we had killed hogs at my in-law's house. Mama had come to help. Of course Mama was in her eighties then, but none the less, she had come to help. We worked all day long and it was way up into the night. Mama was still going strong packing that sausage into jars. We had lost the whole crew from just being plain worn out. She encouraged me and my mother-in-law to keep on going. It is shameful to say, being I was 16 and strong as an ox, but that little women out worked everyone of us that day.

She was a true lover of people, especially children. A mid-wife of the community for many years, she assisted in many birthings and deaths alike. She and her husband, Daddy Bronce cared greatly for their friends and neighbors. When in need the two of them set out to see what they could do to help. In cases where a death had taken place Granddaddy, a furniture maker and carpenter would build the casket; once finished Mama would climb into the casket and make a lining with cloth from her sewing chest. There was never a charge for their services; for you see, they felt this was a part of their christian duty.

Daddy Bronce and Mama Matheson were two truly caring people and are greatly missed by all who knew them.

PICKLING BY THE SIGNS

People in the mountains have always used the signs of the zodiac for almost every undertaking from cutting wood, pulling teeth, to planting potatoes. Following the signs are no less important when it comes to pickling food. In my opinion, following the signs are vital to successful pickling.

For instance, If you pickle in a "bad" sign it will undoubtably show up in the food. Once I had pickled some beans and they smelled rank. When I asked a neighbor lady what I had done wrong she said, "You must have pickled in the wrong sign."

She was right on the mark. I had started my pickling process in the signs of the bowels. Needless to say I had to throw away the whole lot. So I began to go back to my family and neighbors for further explanation of the "signs."

Some of the information I already knew, like when to cut hair, make candy, and cut wood. However, I did learn other things I had heard of when I was a child, but had forgotten. I guess it is true if you don't use it you loose it.

My husband and I had always planted by the signs, and killed our hogs by the signs, although I had forgotten how pickling in the signs worked. When asking people information concerning the signs and pickling there were variations on how to achieve good results.

The moon has four phases: new moon, first quarter, full moon, and last quarter. The moon completes a full cycle in one month and the phases begin again. Within the month there are 12 zodiac signs. A sign will appear at least one day in each month, and may stay a period of two or three days before changing.

Each sign symbolizes a different body part, beginning with the head and ending at the feet. The signs are considered to be masculine or feminine and have a symbolic relationship to fire, water, air, and earth. When pickling the signs to avoid are the bowels, breast, and feet. The most favorable signs are the thighs, knees, and legs.

As for the moon phases, well, there were differing opinions, some folks believe the best phase is the first quarter while others thought the last quarter was better. I know that the signs given to avoid when pickling are accurate.

As for the use of the moon phases, I tried pickling in both phases. They both worked fine, but the pickling done in the first quarter seemed to produce a better product.   Here is my pickling advice: First, obtain a good farmers almanac calender and begin to familiarize yourself with the signs of the zodiac and moon phases.   Begin pickling in the signs of the thighs, knees, or legs, during the first quarter phase of the moon.   Make sure that the water level stays above the food being pickled.

During the new moon phase no additional water should be needed in the crock for the water level will rise with the increasing of the moon until the moon has fulled. Water will decrease in the crock after the full of the moon. Experiment with the signs and moon phases— see what works for you. I think you will be surprised to see how well these old-time methods work.

My husband Kenneth.

CHAPTER SIX

Old-Timey Pickling

Two types of processing exist, long process and short process pickles. To make sweet or sour pickles use non-iodized salt, known as canning salt. Apple cider or white vinegar may be used; it is up to you and your recipe. In certain recipes ground or whole spices may be called for. As a general rule, spices are tied up in a piece of cloth or a homemade cloth bag and removed before being packed. In some recipes alum or household lime (slaked lime) may be called for. These ingredients can be found at the drugstore. Alum or lime can be used to make the pickles crisp, or the addition of a single washed grape leaf in each jar will have the same effect.

To prepare the vegetable, wash thoroughly and allow to dry. Make sure to begin the pickling process within 24 hours after picking; waiting longer will cause hollow or shriveled pickles. Pare, cut, or use whole vegetables as your recipe demands necessary. Pack into crock, large jar, or barrel and cover with brine made of salt, water, and vinegar (vinegar was not always used). To keep vegetables under the brine, weigh them down with a clean plate and place a clean flint rock on the top. A clean white cotton material makes a nice sack to place the vegetable in if you wish to keep the slim away from the vegetable, but it's not necessary.

The room used to pickle in needs to be between 60 and 80 degrees. A daily check should be performed to make sure the brine is always above the vegetable. Remove any scum that forms on top of the brine. If liquid needs to be added, mix together a 1/2 gallon of water, 1/2 cup salt, and 1/2 cup vinegar; pour in the amount needed. Cap off the remainder and set aside to use latter.

Fermented or brined pickles take a long period of time (usually 2 or 3 weeks) to cure before processing. This process allows the pickles to be made in large quantities. Barrels or large crocks are used to contain the cucumbers or other vegetables during the curing time. This process makes the inside of the cucumber firm, tender, and changes the color from green to olive.

When the curing process has completed and the vegetable is fermented, pack the vegetable into clean mason jars, and process in a boiling water bath 15 minutes. Store in a cool dark place.

HOW TO MAKE APPLE CIDER VINEGAR

(Wooden barrels or non-metal containers may be used)

Whole apples (quartered)
or peelings and cores
Cider press or homemade press

Step #1

OPTION A.
    If using whole apples. Wash, quarter, grind, and press apples. Place the juice in a large wooden barrel. Allow the barrel to sit undisturbed until sediment settles in the bottom. Wash out the barrels in which the juice is to be placed with boiling water. Fill the barrel 3/4 full with apple juice. Leave the bung (plug) out . Put a clean loose plug made of cotton in the bung to keep out dirt and insects.

OPTION B.
    If using the peelings and cores. Place peelings and cores into wooden barrel or non-metal container. Fill the container 3/4 full with peel-

ings and cores. Pour hot water over peelings to barely cover. Add 1 cup of sugar to ever 3 gallons of peelings and cores. Mix well. Leave the bung out or container uncovered. Put a clean loose plug made of cotton in the bung to keep dirt and insects out. If using a non-metal container cover the top with a clean white piece of sheeting or a double thickness of cheese cloth. Tie a string securely around the top to keep dirt and insects out.

Step #2

To speed up the process, a cake of compressed yeast may be added or a piece of mother. "Mother" is gel-like particles that form in apple cider vinegar, making a gel like mass that will eventually cover the top. As soon as the alcoholic fermentations cease (which will take several weeks to months), drain out the liquid from container, rinse barrels, and put the vinegar back in again, filling the barrels 3/4 full. Add from 2 to 4 quarts of vinegar which contain "mother" for every 5 gallons of liquid.

Step #3

Store the barrels or non-metal containers in as warm of a place as possible until vinegar is made (usually taking another 6 months). Then after vinegar is made fill the barrels and bung them tight. If containers are used put an air tight lid on to seal.

HONEY VINEGAR (WHITE VINEGAR)

1 quart strained honey
8 quarts warm water

Mix honey and water together in a 3 gallon crock. Tie a piece of white cotton cloth over the top of the crock. Let stand in a warm place until fermentation ceases. Pour vinegar into jars and seal. Makes a nice type of white vinegar.

• CUCUMBER PICKLES •

ALUM PICKLES

Soak 30 small cucumbers overnight in ice cold water to which was added a 1/2 cup of salt. The next morning, remove the cucumbers and wash in cold water. Put cucumbers into hot quart jars and add the following to each jar:

1/8 tsp. powdered alum
1 clove garlic
1 head of fresh dill
1 small hot red pepper

Boil a mixture of 1 quart vinegar, 1 cup salt, and 3 quarts water, fill each jar and seal.

BREAD AND BUTTER PICKLES

1 gallon thinly slices cucumbers
1 hot red pepper
1 hot green pepper
2 large sweet peppers
8 small onions
1 1/2 cups salt

Cover with salt and household lime; let stand over night. Next day wash thoroughly with 3 or 4 changes of cold water. In a large pan or pot bring to a boil:

1 1/2 tsp. turmeric
1/2 tsp. whole cloves
2 Tbsp. celery seed
2 Tbsp. mustard seed
5 cups vinegar

Add cucumber assortment to the mixture. Bring to a rolling boil. Pack into jars leaving 1/4 inch head space and seal.

CRYSTAL CLEAR PICKLES

1 1/2 gallon sliced cucumbers
2 cups household lime
2 gallon cold water

Mix together the first 3 ingredients, let stand over night. Wash cucumbers the next day in 3 or 4 changes of cold water.

2 quart vinegar
1 Tbsp. celery seed
1 Tbsp. ginger
9 cups sugar
1 Tbsp. cloves
3 Tbsp. salt.

Mix latter ingredients and pour cold over cucumbers. Let stand over night, boil 35 minutes, put into jars and seal.

DILL PICKLES #1

20 pounds whole cucumbers
3/4 cup mixed pickling spice
25 heads of fresh dill
8 Tbsp dill seed
1/2 cups salt
2 1/2 cups vinegar
2 1/2 cups water

Mix the spices together and put about half in the bottom of a 5 gallon crock. Put washed whole cucumbers in carefully, so not to bruise. Fill until a couple inches from the top. Place the other half of the mixed spices over the top of the cucumbers. Mix together salt, vinegar, and water to make a brine; then pour over the cucumbers and spices. Weigh down with a clean plate and flint rock. Skim the top when needed. Wait about 21 days until pickled well, then place pickles into jars and seal.

DILL PICKLES #2

3/4 cup sugar   1/2 cup salt
1 quart vinegar   1 quart water
Green or dry dill   Clean grape leaves
3 Tbsp. pickling spice
30 to 40 medium cucumbers
    (cut in half or lengthwise)

Combine sugar, salt, vinegar, and water. Tie spices in a cheese cloth bag, add to vinegar mixture. Simmer 15 minutes. Pack cucumbers into hot jars leaving 1/4 inch head space. Put a head of fresh dill and a clean grape leaf into each jar. Bring brine to a boil and pour over cucumbers, leaving 1/4 inch head space. Adjust caps and seal.

KOSHER METHOD FOR DILL PICKLES

Follow recipe for dill pickles. When packing into jars, add to each jar the following, then adjust caps and seal.

1 clove garlic   1 bay leaf
1/2 tsp. mustard   1 piece hot pepper

LIME PICKLES

2 cups of pickling lime (household lime)
10 lbs. cucumbers sliced crosswise
2 gallons cold water

Place the cucumbers into the lime and water mixture. Let it sit undisturbed overnight (24 hrs). Take out of the mixture and rinse in cold water three or four times until water runs clear. Let the washed cucumbers stand in ice cold water for about 1 1/2 to 2 hours. Remove from water. Combine the following:

10 cups of sugar (5 lb. bag)
2 quarts of vinegar
1/2 cup salt
3 Tbsp mixed pickling spices

Bring mixture to a simmer, then add cucumbers and bring to a full boil for 15 minutes. Put pickles in jars, leaving 1/4 inch head space. Adjust lids and place in a boiling water bath for 15 minutes to seal.

• RELISHES •

CORN SALAD

12 large ears of corn
3 sweet green peppers (chopped)
4 stalks celery (chopped)
4 medium onions (chopped)
2 pimento peppers (chopped)
3 pints vinegar   1 pint sugar
2 tsp. salt   1 tsp. pepper
1 Tbsp. ground mustard

Boil corn on cob for 10 minutes. When cool enough to handle, cut corn off the cob. Mix together all ingredients. Boil 20 minutes, put into jars and seal.

CUCUMBER RELISH

1 gallon chunked cucumbers
4 onions
4 Tbsp. mustard seed
4 cups brown sugar
4 cups vinegar
4 Tbsp. ground horse radish
4 tsp. turmeric
50 whole cloves

Chunk cucumbers, (with peeling left on) peel and slice onions; cover with salt water and let stand 3 hours, then drain. Place spices, vinegar, and sugar in a large pot. Simmer for 15 minutes. Add cucumbers and onions; bring to a boil for 3 minutes, put into sterilized jars and seal.

HOT TOM

1 gallon green bell peppers
                (ground and drained)
2 pints (or more) sweet bell peppers
                (ground and drained)
1 quart onions   *(ground, NOT DRAINED)*
1 1/2 gallon green tomatoes
                (ground & drained)

1/2 cup horse radish *(ground)*
1 tsp. black pepper
5 Tbsp. salt
2 pounds light brown sugar
6 cups white sugar
1/2 gallon vinegar

Mix & boil 30 minutes. Add freshly ground hot pepper to taste when nearly done (Hot pepper loses some strength while cooking). Pack into hot jars and seal.

PEPPER AND APPLE RELISH

12 red sweet peppers
12 green sweet peppers
3 hot red peppers
8 large red apples
15 med. onions
2 pounds of sugar
1 quart vinegar

Chop (do not grind) peppers, apples, and onions. After they have been chopped rather course, place in a vessel and add salt. Cover with boiling water and let stand 20 minutes, then remove water by draining in a colander. Poor sugar and vinegar (add more if needed) over drained ingredients and cook 25 minutes. Put into pint jars and seal.

• PICKLED VEGETABLES •

PICKLED BEETS

4 quarts beets (peeled and cooked)
3 cups onion (thinly sliced)

2 cups sugar	2 sticks cinnamon
1 tsp. whole cloves	1 tsp. whole allspice
1 1/2 tsp. salt	3 1/2 cups vinegar
1 1/2 cups water	

Wash and drain beets. Trim off leafy tops, leaving about 1 1/2 inch of the stem. Bring a large kettle of water to a boil. Place beets into water and cook until tender. Remove the skins from beets and trim ends if necessary. Combine the remaining ingredients into a large pot or kettle. Bring to a boil and let simmer 10 minutes. Add beets to solution and heat through. Remove cinnamon sticks and pack beets with juice into jars and seal.

PICKLED BEANS

Green beans	1 cup vinegar
1 cup salt	1 gallon hot water

String and break beans that will be used. Remove any spots or bad places from the beans. Wash beans well, then cook in a pot with water until they turn their color (beans will become a more olive shade of green). Put the beans in a place to cool overnight. Next day, put drained cooked green beans into a crock. Mix together brine ingredients, pour over cooked beans until covered (May have to mix up more of the solution depending upon the amount of beans being used). Weigh down with a clean plate or saucer and place a clean flint rock on top. Tie a white cloth over the top. Look into the jar daily, if needed skim of scum from the top off liquid. Wait about 21 days until pickled well, then pickled beans may be placed into clean quart jars and sealed.

CHOW CHOW

1 gallon cabbage (chopped fine)
1/2 gallon onions (chopped fine)
1 quart red sweet peppers (chopped fine)
1 quart green sweet peppers (chopped fine)
1/2 gallon green tomatoes (chopped fine)
6 hot banana peppers (chopped course)
1 gallon vinegar
5 pounds brown sugar
4 cups white sugar
1 Tbsp. black pepper
1/2 cup salt

Put all the vegetables and their juice into a large crock (may use individual jars if needed) Pour over vinegar, brown sugar, pepper, and salt; stir well. Stir the contents well each day for 5 days. No need to can this chow chow; it will keep in a stone crock with out sealing.

PICKLED CORN

1 gallon hot water
1 cup vinegar
1 cup salt

Shuck corn and wash well removing silks. Place ears of corn into a large pot of water. Bring to a rolling boil for 10 minutes. Drain water off of cooked corn. Set aside to cool over night. Next day, cut corn off whole from the cob. Put the corn into a large stone crock and pour brine solution over to cover corn. Put a plate on top and weigh down with a flint rock. Cover the top with a clean white cloth and tie securely. Allow to work for about 21 days. May be placed into clean quart jars and sealed. (corn may be pickled on the cob also)

PICKLED BEANS AND CORN

1 gallon hot water
1 cup vinegar
1 cup salt

Pickled beans and corn can be made by mixing together cooked beans and corn. Working them off together in the churn jar following the same guide lines as for pickled beans.

PICKLED EGGS

24 hard-boiled eggs (peeled)
1/2 tsp. whole cloves   2 Tbsp. celery seed
2 Tbsp. mustard seed   1/2 tsp. salt
1/2 cup sugar   1 quart vinegar

Boil eggs and place them immediately into cold water, changing as needed. Remove shells from eggs and rinse in cold water. Let eggs drain, then place into jars. Bring vinegar, sugar, and spices to a boil, turn down heat and let simmer for 20 minutes. Use a strainer to separate the spices from the vinegar solution. Pour the vinegar solution over the eggs and seal. The eggs will be pickled in 14 to 21 days.

PICKLED JERUSALEM ARTICHOKES

A Jerusalem artichoke is a type of perennial sunflower that produces a large tuber. This tuber can be harvested in the fall scraped, cooked, and eaten or may be canned, pickled, or buried. Dig root of the Jerusalem artichoke in autumn. Wash well to remove soil, scrape, and slice. Soak in cold water containing 1/2 cup salt (salt is added to crispen) overnight. The next day rinse pieces with cold water and dry off. Put pieces into clean jars and pour boiling liquid mixture over and seal.

Boiling liquid mixture:
1 quart vinegar   1 pint water *(cont.)*

1 1/2 cups sugar   1/4 cup salt
1 oz. ginger

PICKLED OKRA

3 pounds of small okra pods
Fresh dill weed   Garlic cloves
1/2 cup salt   1 pint vinegar
1 quart water

Wash okra in cold water, drain well. Do not cut okra, leave whole. Pack the okra into pint jars and put a clove of garlic and/or a pod of hot pepper into each jar. Bring brine mixture to a boil and pour into jars containing okra and seal. Will be cured in a few weeks and ready to eat.

PICKLED ONIONS/RAMPS

4 quarts of small whole onions or ramps
1 cup canning salt
2 cups sugar
1/2 tsp. celery seed
1/2 tsp. whole cloves
1/2 tsp. mustard seed
2 quarts vinegar

Clean and peel onions or ramps. Wash in cold water and drain. Place into a large container of ice cold water 1/2 cup salt, add onions or ramps and allow to sit in salt water over night. Drain off water and rinse. Combine sugar, vinegar, and spices in kettle and allow to simmer for 15 minutes. Place onions or ramps into pint jars. Pour hot liquid over and seal.

PICKLED PEPPERS

4 quarts hot banana peppers
(cut into rounds or left whole)
1 1/2 cups salt
1/4 cup sugar
2 cloves garlic
1 1/2 cups water
2 1/2 quarts vinegar
Several pods of hot red pepper

Wash peppers (not hot red peppers) and place into a large container. Mix together 1 1/2 cups of salt into about 1 gallon of ice cold water, pour solution over pickles and let stand over night in a cool place. Bring to a boil sugar, garlic, water, and vinegar, reduce heat and allow to simmer for 15 minutes. Remove garlic from liquid. Pack peppers into pint jars. Pour hot liquid over peppers, add 1 red hot pepper to each jar and seal.

SAUERKRAUT

Select firm heads of cabbage. Remove outside leaves and stalks. Place cabbage into a large container and chop good. Have waiting a clean, large churn jar (usually 5 gallon size). Pack the chopped cabbage into the churn jar alternating layers of cabbage and salt (1/2 cup salt to 1 gallon chopped cabbage). Do not add any water, the kraut will make it's own juice. After the churn jar is filled to within 3 inches of the top, place and clean plate or saucer on top. Then weigh down the plate with a clean flint rock. The cabbage will make into sauerkraut under brine. Cover the top with a clean white cloth or cheesecloth; tie into place with a string. Let cabbage stand about 21 days or until it gets sour enough to suit taste. After the sauerkraut has made you may remove the kraut from the churn jar and place into pint or quart jars to seal. Leaving the kraut in the churn jar will not hurt, you may remove the kraut as needed and replace the cloth. (Kraut left in the churn jar will become a little dark over time.)

SAUERKRAUT IN QUART JARS

1 gallon hot water   1 cup canning salt
1 cup vinegar

Pack chopped cabbage into jars. Pour mixture slowly over cabbage and place lids and rings securely (not to tight) onto jars. Put jars where they can work over (jar will spew out fluid during the fermentation process). It will be ready in 3 or 4 weeks, then tighten lid and rings again; they will loosen when cabbage is working.

SQUASH PICKLES

10 cups of sliced yellow
    crooked neck squash
6 med. onions (thin sliced)
1/2 cup sweet green peppers (chopped)
1/4 cup salt

Soak sliced squash, sliced onion, and sweet green peppers in ice cold water containing 1/4 cup salt over night.

2 1/2 cups vinegar   4 1/2 cups sugar
1 tsp. celery seed   1 tsp. mustard seed
1 tsp. turmeric

Rinse and drain squash, onion, and peppers the next day. Place all remaining ingredients into a large pot and simmer. Put squash, onion, and peppers into pint jars. Pour hot brine solution over and seal.

• PICKLED FRUITS •

PICKLED CRAB APPLES

Sound crab apples (do not pare)
1 quart vinegar   1 quart sugar
1 Tbsp. cinnamon   1 Tbsp. cloves
1 tsp. allspice   1 tsp. mace

Mix together vinegar, sugar, and spices in a

large vessel. Bring to a boil, thus making a spiced syrup. Remove from heat and cool. Add crab apples to the cooled mixture and heat slowly, being careful not to burst the fruit. Remove from heat, cover and let the apples and syrup stand over night. Place cold fruit into jars, cover with syrup and seal.

PICKLED FOX GRAPES

Pick about 4 pounds of fox grapes
1 cup sugar
1 cup cider vinegar
1 Tbsp. chopped wild ginger root
2 cinnamon sticks
1 tsp. whole cloves

Wash the grapes and remove the stems. Place the grapes and other ingredients into a pot and cook over medium heat until grapes become soft. Mash the grapes up good. Let the grapes sit until the seeds settle in the bottom of the pot. Drain off the top, leaving the seeds. Cook until thick. Adjust lids and seal.

PICKLED PEACHES

10 pounds peeled peach halves
5 pounds light brown sugar
1 quart vinegar
1 Tbsp. ground cloves
1 piece ginger root
4 whole sticks of cinnamon

Prepare a boiling syrup of sugar, vinegar, and spices. Add peaches to syrup and cook until tender, (using a toothpick prick fruit to test) do not over cook. Allow the fruit to stand over night in covered kettle. Next day pack into jars and seal.

WATERMELON RIND PICKLE

10 pounds of watermelon rind, cooked in clear water until tender. Drain for 5 hours. Make a syrup of the following:

1 quart vinegar	2 lbs. sugar
1/2 oz. cloves	1 oz. cinnamon

Boil syrup and spices. Drop in the watermelon rind, and heat thoroughly. Place rind and syrup mixture into jars and seal.

"My son Bronce is a real mountain man; he shore can fill a game bag."

CHAPTER SEVEN

Tame Meat or Wild Game

The mountain range in the Western North Carolina region at one time was densely forested. The mighty chestnut, oak, pine, and poplar groves occupied the territory; at higher elevations majestic spruce-fir stands were seen for miles. A wide assortment of shrubs and herbs were within the forests. With rich soils and on average rainfall between 40 and 80 inches annually, the forests and valley floors were abundant sources of food for animal and human alike. Animals were of great economic importance, ranging form the smallest of species such as rabbit or squirrel to the larger black bear, dear, or wild hog. There were countless varieties of birds found year round, with wild turkey being a favored delicacy. Numerous fish, reptiles, and insects inhabited the range.

Farming was of great importance to mountain folk. Small plots of land called gardens grew vegetable crops; which were harvested and stored for winter use. Large fields of corn were grown to be used as feed for the livestock. Hogs were a very important animal to the mountaineer, due to the fact that hogs were not hard to raise and almost every part of a hog could be used. Chickens were among other foul used as a source of meat and fresh eggs. Cows too, were a source of food—an old stock prized for meat and milk producing ability was the Red Debin. Although, some families insisted on owning only Guernsey or Jersey cows. For most mountain folk trading was a common occurrence used to obtain a necessary commodity; whether it be animals, seed, food, or services.

The Mountaineer's are not merely people of the past: They live in the present and plan for the future like anyone else in our modern world. Change and adaptation are a part of their heritage, a ever persistent theme in their history. While living in a harsh environment, with very little means—when all odds were surely against them—they survived. The present day mountaineer's have hope by drawing strength and inspiration from their ancestors as they look ahead to the future.

PREPARING MEAT FOR CANNING

Meats should not be canned until all of the animal heat has left, which usually takes between 3 and 24 hours after killing. Soak meat in a brine solution containing 1/4 cup salt to 1 gallon of water. Choice jars for canning meat are wide mouth quarts, the wide mouth jar makes it easier to put meat into the jars and makes removal easier too. Meats may be precooked or packed raw.

CANNING MEAT

RAW MEATS CUT INTO CHUNKS, CUBES, OR STRIPS INCLUDE: Beef, pork, lamb, venison, bear, ground hog.

After the meat has chilled and been soaking in a brine solution for an hour. Rinse well. Remove the bones and cut the meat into chunks, cubes, or strips.

RAW PACK
Place meat into jars, leaving 1 inch of head space. Add 1 tsp. salt to each quart. For meats

packed raw, DO NOT ADD LIQUID. Meats packed raw make their own liquid while processing. Wipe tops of jars clean of grease, liquid, and meat particles. Adjust lids and process.

HOT PACK

Cook the meat until rare by boiling, roasting, or frying in a small amount of fat. Pack hot into quart jars, leaving 1 inch head space. Add 1 tsp. salt per quart. Add boiling broth, or 3 to 4 Tbsp. hot grease to each quart jar. Wipe tops of jars off with a damp cloth to remove any grease or meat particles. Adjust lids and process.

GROUND OR CHOPPED MEAT INCLUDE: Beef, lamb, bear, venison, sausage.

After the meat has chilled and been soaking in a brine solution for an hour. Rinse well. Remove the bones, if fat is needed add fat before grinding. Grind the meat on a meat grinder. Seasonings may be added at this time such as salt, pepper, and sage (use sage sparingly as it becomes strong when canned). Mix the spices well with hands. Make balls or patties. Cook meat until lightly browned or 3/4 of the way done. Pack balls or patties into clean quart jars, leaving 1 inch of head space.

HOT PACK ONLY

HOT PACK WITHOUT ADDED LIQUID: For precooked meats pack hot into jars, leaving 1 inch head space. Add 3 to 4 Tbsp. of grease to each quart of ground or chopped meat (sausage). Adjust lids and process.

HOT PACK WITH ADDED LIQUID: Add hot meat broth, leaving 1 inch of head space. Adjust lids and process.

CANNING FOWL, RABBIT, AND SQUIRREL

RAW MEATS WITH OR WITHOUT BONE INCLUDE: Tame meats include chicken, turkey, duck, goose, and rabbit. Wild meats include ruffled grouse, wild turkey, duck, rabbit and squirrel. After the meat has chilled and been soaking in a brine solution for 1 hour. Rinse well. Remove excess fat. May be canned with the bones or without.

WITH BONES IN:

HOT PACK OR RAW PACK: Pack meat into clean quart jars, leaving 1 inch head space. Add 1 tsp. salt to each quart jar. For meats packed raw, DO NOT ADD LIQUID. Meats packed raw make their own juice while processing. Wipe jars tops clean of grease, liquid, or meat particles. Adjust lids and process.

WITHOUT BONES:

HOT PACK OR RAW PACK: Cook the meat until about two thirds done, by frying, baking or boiling. Pack hot into quart jars, leaving 1 inch head space. Add 1 tsp. salt to each quart jar. Add 3 to 4 Tbsp. hot liquid or grease into each quart jar. Wipe tops of jars off with a damp cloth to remove grease and meat particles. Adjust lids and process.

CORNED BEEF

Remove beef from the brine. After beef has been corned for the correct amount of time. Soak for 2 hours in cold water, changing the water once. Place the corned beef in a large pot and boil slowly for 30 minutes. Remove meat and put into cold water. Cut into small pieces and pack tightly into clean quart jars. Adjust lids and seal.

TROUT

RAW PACK ONLY
Clean fish, cut off heads, fins, and tails. Soak for 1 hour in water containing 1/4 cup salt. Rinse thoroughly in cold water. Leave trout whole if small; cut larger trout into chunks that will fit lengthwise into pint jars only, leaving 1/2 inch head space. Drain water off for 5 to 10 minutes. Add 1/2 tsp. salt to each pint. Adjust lids and process.

SMOKED TROUT

Cut smoked fish into lengths that will fit into jars, leaving 1 inch of head space. DO NOT ADD LIQUID. Adjust lids and process.

• OLD FASHION MEAT STORAGE •

If a family did not have a crock to put their sausage in they would take field corn and prepare casings for the sausage. Corn shuck casings were prepared by removing the ear of corn, washing the shucks, and then dried in the sun or near a fire inside the house. Sausage was then packed into corn shucks and tied with corn fodder, bear grass, or a string around the end to close. It was then hung from the smokehouse joists for curing.

Sausage was once prepared for storage by frying 3/4 done and then placed into crocks, after which hot grease was poured on top. Thus sealing the sausage. A clean, white piece of cloth was then dipped in bees wax and tied around the top. Once the crock was prepared it was set in the spring house to stay where it was cool. When sausage was needed the cloth covering was removed and the sausage taken out.

After canning jars came in to existence they became storage vessels for sausage as well. Here's how it was done: Prepare the sausage for cooking, fry until 3/4 done and place into jars. Pour about 4 tablespoons of hot grease over the sausage. Adjust lids and turn the jars upside down to cool. When the grease cools it seals the jars. Jars are then stored in a cool place.

CHAPTER EIGHT

From the Drying Shed
*"Our family and another family put up
42 bushes of apples last year."*

SUN DRYING METHOD

Before the days of canning jars, mountaineer's dried a wide variety of fruits
and vegetables. Drying was accom-
plished with help from the sun. Drying food
was very economical and still is today. There
are no requirements for expensive materials;
only consecutive warm sunny days.

In dry weather a clean, white sheeting material was taken outside and laid upon a waist
high wooden-slatted scaffold; which had been
constructed to promote good air flow, which is
essential in drying food. The fruit or vegetable

was prepared by peeling, coring, and slicing. The apple peelings were usually saved to make jelly or vinegar out of. The fruit or vegetable was then placed into a pretreatment solution, later removed, rinsed and placed upon the covered scaffold. If available, a thin piece of sheeting material or cheesecloth was laid over the fruit. Bees, especially yellow jackets are drawn to the drying scaffold. Bees will not harm the fruit if left uncovered; covering the fruit is a personal preference. Turn the food occasionally, this will allow more even drying. Now it is left up to the sun to draw out the moisture.

Other folks dry their food upon a drying rock. This rock serves as a warm site to lay food without the need to build a scaffold. A clean sheeting material is always placed under the fruit. Not only does it keeping debris away from food, but it is used to transfer food in and out of the house daily and when threatening weather prevails. The food is brought in each night before the dew falls and returned outside the next day after the dew has dried. This routine is followed until the fruit or vegetable is dry, usually taking about 3 or 4 days. In case of rainy weather, bring food indoors and continue to dry by fireside or oven. It may be returned outside the next day weather permitting.

DRYING SHEDS

It was important to have a place to dry food. Most homes had a limited amount of space.

Thus a perfect remedy for such problems was to use what they did have. The smokehouse converted nicely into a drying shed during the drying season. The smokehouse was used not only as a place to cure meat, but to smoke the meat as well. The building usually had space between the boards which offered ventilation, and in summer was very warm inside. Food could be strung and hung up or placed on white oak splits and placed crosswise the joists to dry. It was common to find medicinal herbs, vegetables, and fruits hanging from the joists and roots drying on the board shelving that line the walls.

The front or back porch became a popular place to dry, as well as the attic. It was not so much that a "special" area had to be used for this purpose. Instead, it was that when a need arose, there must be a remedy. A solution was devised from what materials a family had. So out of necessity, problems were solved. This was true for whatever dilemma was at hand. That is why some families had a drying rock; while other families used a scaffold, drying shed, or porch. The ultimate goal was to dry food to feed their families through the barren months of winter.

FIRESIDE AND OVEN DRYING

If rainy weather is apparent, do not attempt to sun dry food. Use the fireside or oven drying methods. The fireside method consists of drying food near a fire on the floor or by making a scaffold from boards to place near the fire. Caution should be taken when placing sheeting material or food close to the fire. When indoors it is not necessary to place a piece of cloth over the food, this will only trap moisture. Turning the fruit or vegetable over often is required, so food will not mold.

The oven drying method is similar. Place food on cookie sheets or other usable pans and set in the oven with the door ajar. Turn or stir food occasionally. The heat is kept at a low temperature between 90 and 130 degrees. Oven drying takes from between 12 and 24 hours. When deemed necessary the food may be removed from the heat source, but processing must continue the next day.

When done vegetables will be brittle and the fruit leathery, regardless of the method used to dry foods. The most important factors in successful food drying are the following: to have good air circulation, turn or stir foods occasionally, protect food from the dampness of night and morning dew, and to make sure food is dry before storing. Remember, vegetables will be brittle and fruits will be leathery.

DRY FOOD STORAGE

When storing dried foods be sure they are indeed dry and completely cool. If moisture filled foods or warm foods from which heat is escaping is stored, the result will be molded food. To store dried foods a piece of clean cloth can be made into a sack and used to place the food in or a clean pillow case will do nicely. A clean glass jar or stone crock works good also.

TO RECONSTITUTE DRIED FOODS

A word of caution, dried foods will double or triple in bulk after soaking, so it doesn't take much to make a serving. The drying process reduces the amount of moisture dramatically, thus condensing the food item. Soak the desired amount of dried food in cold water to cover until softened. Do not add sugar or salt to rehydrating food until last 10 minutes of process. Prepare food as usual.

PRETREATMENT SOLUTIONS

Lemon solution
1 cup lemon juice to 1 gallon of water

Salt solution
3 Tbsp. salt to 1 gallon of water

Salt and Vinegar solution
2 Tbsp. salt and 2 Tbsp. vinegar into
1 gallon cold water

A pretreatment solution of either lemon, salt, or salt and vinegar is set aside to place fruit or vegetable into. Once the fruit or vegetable has been peeled and seed removed, the pieces are cut into the desired rings or slices and placed into the solution. The solution keeps the fruit or vegetable from turning dark. Fruits are usually dipped into a lemon, salt, or salt and vinegar solution. Vegetables are mostly dipped into a salt solution, but a solution was not always used on vegetables. Lemon juice dipping came much latter than the former methods. Vinegar and salt solutions act in the same way as lemon juice, both being acidic.

APPLES

Wash and peel apples. Apples may be cored and sliced into rings or quartered, cored, and cut into thin slices. Put the slices or rings into a lemon or salt pretreatment solution as described earlier. Place fruit out in the sun to dry or run the rings onto a sassafras limb or white oak split and hang from the joists (two chairs may be used to hang the apples between).

BEANS "LEATHER BREECHES"

Pick the beans and bring in from the garden. Rinse the beans in cold water if needed. Remove the strings from the beans. Break into pieces or leave whole. Begin to string them on a large eyed needle filled with a long piece of strong twine. Hang the beans out of the sun, on a porch or in a drying shed, this helps to retain their color better. After dried, leave beans on the string and place in a homemade sack or pillow case. Green beans can be broke into pieces and laid out in the sun if desired.

BEANS "SHELLIES"

Beans that are to be shelled out are called "shellies". These beans are latter used for soupy beans. A variety prized for shellies are the October Beans and Pole Beans. To shell out beans string the beans and pull the hull apart. Remove the beans within by shelling into a dishpan or other container. Lay the shellies out onto drying trays or in baskets to dry. Shake the beans around to allow for good air flow and even drying. After completely dry, put the beans into a cloth sack or tightly closed tin.

CABBAGE

Select firm heads of cabbage, Remove the outside layers and feed to the hogs. Quarter the cabbage, remove the inside stalks and discard. Spread the leaves on board shelf inside the drying shed out of direct sunlight. When dry store in a clean cloth sack.

CORN

Select corn that is in the milk stage. Husk, silk, and trim out bad places or ends, then wash the corn in cold water. Place the ears of corn into a large kettle and bring to a boil. Boil corn for 10 minutes to set the milk. After cooling cut the corn off the cob twice. As for making cream corn. To dry spread the corn out on trays in the sun until dry.

CORN "WHOLE"

Select corn that is in the milk stage. Pull the shucks back and tie with a piece of fodder or a string. Hang the ear of corn in the sun until dry and hard. Store inside in a wooden box, sack, or hanging up.

HOMINY

After the hominy has been made, allow it to cool and drain over night. The next day place the hominy outside in the sun, stirring occasionally to allow even drying. After dry store in homemade sacks or pillow cases. May be salted and eaten dry as a nut substitute.

NUTS

Crack nuts and remove the nut meats. Put the nut meats into jars. Adjust the lids and process in an oven at 225 degrees for 45 minutes. Or nuts may be stored in a dry place within their shell.

OKRA

Select small to medium pods of okra. Wash

in cold water. Cut the ends off the pods and slice into small rounds. Dry in the sun. Put the dried okra into sacks for storage.

ONIONS

Collect onions from the garden after the tops have died down, preferably during an afternoon when the ground is good and dry. The onions are then bound at the top by bunches and tied with a string or piece of fodder. Then bunches of onions are hung up on the porch or in the drying shed until dry. Store hanging up in a warm place so not to freeze.

PEPPERS

Collect peppers when mature. String them onto a large eyed needed with a piece of long strong twine. Hang the peppers in a dry, warm place until brittle. Leave on the string to store hanging up or in a muslin bag. To dry sweet bell pepper, half the peppers, remove the stems, and seeds. Slice into narrow strips or small pieces and dry in the sun.

PEACHES

Select firm, ripe peaches. Wash peaches and dip into boiling water for about 1 minute, then plunge into cold water. Peels will be loose, slip them from the peaches. Cut the peaches into half and remove the seed. Cut into 1/4 inch slices. Place sliced peaches into a pre-treatment solution as they are cut. Dry, turning occasionally until leathery and pliable. Store in clean, cloth sack or pillow case.

PUMPKIN

Cut pumpkin or candy roaster into rings. Remove the seeds and peeling. Hang the rounds on a stick crosswise the joists of the drying shed. When completely dry put the dried rounds in a clean sack to store.

SWEET POTATOES

Select good firm sweet potatoes. Wash and place into a large pot of water. Bring the water to a boil and cook the sweet potatoes until done. Remove the outside peeling and slice into 1/4 inch slices. Dry in the sun. When completely dry store as with other dried foods.

WILD BERRIES

Wash berries. Place berries in the sun on a wooden board or nonmetal tray. Once the berries begin to dry mix with hands, so they will dry evenly. Store in clean, cloth sack.

DRYING PLANTS FOR TEAS

Collect whole plants to be dried after the dew has dried. Gather the bunches by the cut ends and tie with a twine. Hang upside down in the drying shed. When dry the leaves and stems may be crushed or ground into tea. The drying room provides a dark, warm, ventilated place for the plants to dry, thus retaining most of their color.

DRYING ROOTS

Collect the roots in the appropriate season. Wash the roots well to remove dirt and debris. Lay the roots onto board shelf in the drying room. When dry, the roots will be hard and brittle.

FRUIT LEATHER

5 cups applesauce (or other fruit)
1/2 cup sugar (honey can be substituted)
Spices may be used
(for apple leather 1/4 tsp. cinnamon)

Mix fruit sauce, sugar, and spices together. Cook to the consistency of thick oatmeal, stirring constantly. Spread the thick fruit sauce 1/4 inch thick onto shallow pans. Place in a warm dry area covered with a piece of cheese cloth for about two weeks or until dry enough to peel from the pan or bake in a 150 degree oven, with the door ajar (slightly open) 4 hours or until dry.

If drying in the sun, process will take about 2 days if temperature is around 80 degrees. Be sure to cover the fruit sauce with a thin piece of cheese cloth to keep out insects.

When the fruit leather is dry enough to lift from the pan, place on sticks so that air can circulate around both sides. When fruit leather is no longer sticky dust with a little arrowroot powder or corn starch. Wrap each sheet in brown paper and store in a cool, dark place.

BLEACHING FRUIT

Select ripe, firm fruit. Peel, remove seed, and cut into 1/4 inch pieces. Spread the fruit (so not to touch) into an oak split basket or onto wooden slats. Put into a wooden tub, hickory coals which have no smoke or smell left to them. Sprinkle about 2 tsp. of sulfur per pound of fresh fruit onto the coals. Hang the basket of fruit in the top of the tub. Cover the barrel with a clean piece of sheeting; covering the tub holds in the sulfur fumes. Allow the fruit to stay in the covered tub, undisturbed for about 25 to 30 minutes. Fruit will be bright and shiny when done. Remove the fruit from the tub and store in crock jars. Covering with a clean piece of material tied over the jar.

MOONSHINE

THESE ARE THE THINGS YOU WILL NEED
TO MAKE CORN WHISKEY OF THE DAY
WHEN LABOR WAS SO HARD TO FIND
MOUNTAIN LIFE IS HERE TO STAY

A STILL TO MAKE AND COMPLETE
ALL THE ITEMS YOU MUST REAP
SILVER SOLDER, COPPER PIPE, AND SHEETING
THE WOODEN BARRELS ARE VERY DEEP

ROCKS ARE MANY AND SO CHEAP
JUST WAITING TO PICK THEM UP
ADD MUD AND WATER TO MAKE MORTAR
A FIREBOX YOU'D CONSTRUCT

NOW YOU MUST COLLECT
WATER FLOWING AND WOOD WHICH TO BURN
THESE THINGS I'M TELLING
ARE INEVITABLE FOR YOU TO LEARN

CORN IN BUSHEL'S, SUGAR TOO
MEAL IN A SACK
ARE INGREDIENTS THAT YOU GATHER
NONE OF THEM MUST YOU LACK

BURY CORN BENEATH MANURE HEAP
IT WILL SURELY SPROUT
PUT IT IN A GRINDER, MIX WITH SUGAR
IT WILL BE QUITE STOUT

ADD COLD WATER FROM A SPRING
COVER WITH MEAL TO STAY
GO HOME FOR A WHILE NOW
WORK OFF ANOTHER DAY

START A FIRE IN THE BOX
EARLY IN THE DAY
READY NOW TO CAP OFF THE TOP
WITH GENUINE RED CLAY

FILL THE CONDENSER WITH COLD WATER
THE WORM COILED WITHIN
NOW YOUR READY, WITH ROLLING LAUGHTER
YOU MAY NOW BEGIN

RUNNING CLEARLY AND NEARLY READY
LET MOST OF IT DRIP OUT
HURRY NOW, FRUIT JARS TO GARNER
ALMOST TIME TO FILL, NO DOUBT

PULL OUT THE FIRE, SO NOT TO SCORCH
THE BACKINGS YOU WILL USE
TO WORK AGAIN, JUST ADD SUGAR
COOK THIS BATCH A NEW

MIX THE STRONG AND THE LATTER
FOR A DRINK OF FINE ARRAY
SHAKE AND WATCH THE BEADS A DANCING
HALF AND HALF, DO NOT DELAY

NOW A DRINK SO FINE AND TRUE
GUARANTEE TO FIX YOUR ILLS
DRINK IT SLOWLY, SIPPING BOLDLY
OR IT WILL BURN YOUR GILLS

NOW YOU HAVE LEARNED AN ART
FROM OLD TIMES GONE BY
USE IT WISELY OR WILL SMITE THEE
UNTIL THE DAY YOU DIE

—lesa w. postell

CHAPTER NINE

Juices And The Like
"Ya gotta have something to wet your whistle."

In the mountain counties of Western North Carolina, not to long ago it was a hard place to rear a family, due to the lack of jobs. Most of the jobs revolved around the logging industry, then came construction work which was referred to as road jobs. The logging camps and road houses were considered "rough" places, giving way to unlawful activities. Some of the men left their families at home and went away to work these jobs. Those men who went to work on public jobs had to leave their wives and families at home to tend to the farms. Most of the time the wages that were made was very little compared to the labor given. Men sometimes made moonshine to help provide money for their families. As moonshining became a lucrative business, the government wanted tax from the sales. Soon revenuers, which were government agents came into the area to control the sale of alcohol. Moonshine, was sometimes referred to as corn squeezings or scorpion juice. This powerful alcoholic drink was used for medical purposes, a pleasurable drink and as an additive to preserve plants for home remedies.

Many other drinks were made from wild plants and roots which may have been considered a tonic or just a refreshing drink. The drinks which were made from plants were known mostly as teas, although others were referred to as coffee. Berries were plentiful from spring through early autumn. Berries were used to make refreshing beverages, as well as wines. Apple trees were found at nearly every farmstead. Apple cider, a favored drink was made in the fall once the apples were sweet and ripe. And of course there were cows—most families had a least one milk cow. The cow provided milk, butter, buttermilk, and cheese.

Mountain folks had a wide variety of drinks of which to consume. Working hard in the hills from daylight till dark brought on a powerful thirst. Sometimes vinegar mixed with cold spring water and honey was used to quench thirst and return energy. Mountaineers knew that "you gotta have something to wet your whistle." Water was the most common drink used, followed by coffee, buttermilk and sweet milk. Herbal teas and wild coffee substitutes were a special treat treasured by all. Within this chapter you will visit many of the home-made teas, juices, and coffees valued by the mountaineers of the past and the present.

CAUTION: ANY OF THE WILD PLANTS MEN-TIONED MUST BE POSITIVELY IDENTIFIED, DO NOT GATHER PLANTS THAT YOU ARE NOT FAMILIAR WITH.

• COFFEE AND COFFEE SUBSTITUTES •

BOILED COFFEE

Rinse coffee pot with hot water. Measure coffee into the pot, put 1 Tbsp. Coffee for each cup of water. Place water into the pot. Heat rapidly to boiling. Boil 3 minutes. Clear with 1/4 cup of cold water to settle the grounds. Strain and serve.

BOILED COFFEE WITH EGG

1 heaping Tbsp. coffee to each cup of water
1 extra Tbsp. coffee for the pot
1 tsp. slightly beaten egg white
1 cup boiling water

Place the coffee in a clean pot. Stir in egg white. Add just enough boiling water to cover, whip well with a fork. Add boiling water, cover with a tight lid. Place over heat, slowly bring to a brisk boil. Boil 3 minutes. Remove pot from heat. Pour 3 Tbsp. cold water down the spout. Let stand for 3 or 4 minutes. Stain and serve.

CHICORY COFFEE

Gather the roots of chicory. Wash and peel. Roast the roots slowly in the oven or near the fire until brown. Allow the roots to cool and grind up. Use the roasted roots as a coffee substitute or to stretch out store-bought coffee. Use 1 tsp. ground root to each cup of water. Boil 4 minutes.

DANDELION COFFEE

Gather the roots of the common dandelion. Wash and peel. Roast in a slow oven until brown. Allow the roots to cool and grind up. Use 1 tsp. of ground root to each cup of water. Boil for 4 minutes. Use in the place of coffee.

• HERBAL TEA'S •

BIRCH BARK TEA

Gather twigs of the Black Birch tree. Break into pieces about 3 inches long. Rinse under cold water. Place twigs in a pot and pour boiling water over them. Allow to step for 20 minutes. Strain, sweeten, and serve hot. Tastes like wintergreen.

HEMLOCK TEA

Collect the branch tips (needled) of the Eastern Hemlock tree. Place a scant handful in a pot. Cover with boiling water and allow to steep a few minutes. Strain, sweeten, and serve hot.

MOUNTAIN MINT TEA

Collect mint leaves in the morning after the dew has dried. When using dried leaves, place 1 tsp. dried mint leaves to each cup of water. For fresh leaves, place leaves at the rate of 2 tsp. to each cup of water. Put measured water and leaves in a kettle. Bring water to a boil. Boil 3 minutes, remove from heat and steep about 15 or 20 minutes. Strain, sweeten and serve hot or cold. *Leaves and stems may be collected and hung upside down to dry in a well ventilated, warm, dry place.*

NEW JERSEY TEA

Collect the leaves and dry thoroughly. Crush leaves and place in a homemade tea bag. Bring water to a boil. Remove from heat add tea bag. Steep a few minutes, sweeten and serve hot. Use like commercial tea.

SASSAFRAS TEA

An early spring tonic and beverage to be

gathered and drank is sassafras. Gather small sapling, pull up by the roots, or dig down beside a tree and chop off a section of root. Not only can you use the roots, but the branches too. Wash the roots, removing dirt and debris, and drain. At this stage you may dry the root for future use or continue to make a tea. Beat the large roots into a pulp; the smaller roots and twigs can be broken to fit into a pot. Cover with water and bring to a boil for 15 minutes. Remove from heat and allow tea to cool. The longer the tea is allowed to sit undisturbed the stronger the tea. Strain, sweeten to taste with honey and serve. May be drunk hot or cold. Save the roots to be used in another batch latter.

SPICEWOOD TEA

Gather the twigs in early spring, don't strip off the flowers. Put a hand full of twigs into a pot of water. Bring water to a boil for 15 minutes. Remove from heat and allow to sit until steeping is done. Strain, sweeten, and serve.

SUMAC LEMONADE

Collect Staghorn Sumac tops (red horns). Bring water to a boil, remove from heat. Add sumac horns to the hot water and allow to steep. Strain through a cloth to remove the fuzzy little particles and sweeten. Serve cold.

WILD APRICOT DRINK

Gather "old field" apricots. Wash fruit in cold water. Split the fruit open and put into a pot of boiling water to which a pinch of baking soda is added (loosens seed from meat). Boil 5 minutes, strain, and sweeten. Drink cold.

• JUICES •

Choose ripe fruit, remove stems, and debris. Wash carefully in cold water. Quarter larger fruits. Place fruit into a large kettle and add fruit. Mash the fruit well, Add just enough water to barely cover. Simmer the fruit in a covered kettle, do not boil. Cook slowly until the fruit is very soft, about 10 minutes. Strain juice by placing a clean four sack, clean white cloth, jelly bag, or double thickness of cheese cloth onto a strainer with a large container below to catch the juice. If jelly is to be made with the juice do not squeeze the cloth bag. Simply let it run into container freely. The jelly made from this juice will be clear. The remaining pulp can be used to make fruit butter or jam. If the juice is a general run for drinking purposes only, squeeze the two ends of the bag or folded cloth in opposite directions to release larger quantity of juice. Sugar may be added at the rate of 1/2 cup per quart at this time, unless juice is used latter to make jelly then do not add sugar. Fill the jars, leaving 1/2 inch head space. Wipe jar rims with a clean, damp cloth. Adjust lids and seal. To seal place jars of fruit juice in a boiling water bath for 15 minutes, see tomatoes for time, they take longer. Upon opening, notice that sediment will have settled in the bottom of the jars, of the general run juice. It's fine, just shake it up and pour into a pitcher. If sugar was omitted before canning it may be added now. Juice may be diluted to suit taste, unless using apple cider as a hot drink; it's your preference, experiment.

APPLE CIDER (FRESH HOMEMADE)

Sweet and tart apples *(at least 1 bushel)*
Cider press *(if homemade a grinder,*
               and press are needed)
Wash tub *(to wash apples in)*
Knifes *(for quartering apples)*
Cheese cloth *(to strain the cider)*
Large container *(to catch the cider in)*
Other clean vessels *(to put scrap*
              in or hold the cider in)
Clean containers *(to pour cider*
              into for storage)
Canning equipment *(if cider is to be canned)*

Select sweet and tart apples to blend together for the best apple cider. Prepare equipment by washing and rinsing the cider mill. Then grease all metal working parts of the cider mill with vegetable oil or small application of cooking lard. Wash apples in a tub of cold water. Place a cutting board on top of the mill if room is available. Quarter apples and drop into the hopper of the grinder, smaller apples may be put in whole.

Continue to grind quartered apples in the hopper, grinding until the slatted oak tub beneath is full of ground apples. Place a large bucket under the spout. Place a doubled piece of cheese cloth or other clean white cloth over bucket and secure. This will allow you to strain the cider while it is pouring into the bucket, thus saving a step latter. Move slatted oak tub under the press and begin to tighten the pressing screw. Apply pressure slow and steady. Cider will begin to flow out the spout and into the cloth covered bucket below.

When the apples have been pressed to the point that no more cider flows, remove slatted tub. If the bucket is full of strained cider, carefully remove the cloth and pour cider into a holding pan and cover. If the bucket is not yet full continue on. Once the oak-slatted tub has been removed, pour out the discarded apple waste called pomace. This may be saved for making vinegar latter.

If vinegar is to be made of the pomace, put into a clean vessel, otherwise throw away. The process begins over again until desired amount of cider has been made. Clean equipment and store cider. Apple cider may be served cold or hot. To preserve apple cider you may freeze or can.

APPLE CIDER

For the best flavor use fresh cider that is made from sweet and tart apples. Pour the fresh cider into a large pot and heat to simmering, not boiling. Skim the top off if needed. Ladle cider into quart or half gallon jars and seal.

MULLED CIDER

1 quart apple cider
1/2 tsp. cloves
2 cinnamon sticks
1 heaping Tbsp. brown sugar (if desired)

Heat apple cider until simmering, add spice, allow to simmer for 20 minutes. Remove spices, add brown sugar if desired or drink plain.

GRAPE JUICE

Wash sound grapes. Put into a large vessel and cover with water. Heat slowly and follow the directions given at the beginning of this chapter for making fruit juice. Strain, add sugar if desired (1/2 cup per quart or 1 cup per gallon). Ladle into quart or half gallon jars and seal.

QUICK GRAPE JUICE

Wash grapes carefully in cold water and remove stems. Put 1 cup washed grapes into each clean quart jar. Add 1/2 cup sugar to each jar and fill with boiling water and seal.

OTHER FRUIT JUICES

When canning berries or fruits such as blackberries, peaches, etc., simply reserve the juice and add water to make a refreshening drink.

TOMATO JUICE

Wash ripe tomatoes in cold water. Trim ends of tomatoes and remove blemishes. Quarter tomatoes, placing them into a large cooker containing a small amount of water. Heat until simmering, stirring to prevent sticking. When tomatoes are soft, remove from heat. Press through a fine sieve or food mill collecting the juice in a large container below.

Cook juice to boiling point, simmer 5 minutes. Salt or sugar may be added at the rate of 1 tsp. of each to every quart of juice and seal. Tomato juice takes longer to seal than other juices.

VEGETABLE JUICE DRINK

1/2 bushel tomatoes	2 carrots
2 celery stalks	2 green peppers
1 medium onion	1 Tbsp. salt
1/4 cup lemon juice	

Wash vegetables and drain. Prepare vegetables by removing cores, blossom ends and blemishes. Cut vegetables in quarters or slices. Place all the ingredients into a large kettle. Bring to a boil, reduce heat and simmer for 20 minutes. Press through a food mill. Return the vegetable juice to a boil. Ladle into hot jars, leaving 1/4 inch head space. Process 40 minutes in a boiling water bath (longest item used, tomatoes).

• MILK •

MILK (CANNED)

After straining fresh cows milk, let it stand until the animal heat leaves. Pour into clean jars, leaving 1/2 inch head space. Process milk in a pressure canner for 10 minutes at 10 pounds of pressure.

• WINE •

ELDERBERRY WINE

Mix together 1 quart of elderberry juice and 1 quart of warm water. Add 2 pints of brown sugar and mix well. Place into a stone crock. After about a week the fermentation slows down and eventually stops, then wine may be bottled and sealed in glass jars.

GRAPE WINE

    5 pounds grapes or other fruits
            such as blackberries, or apples
    5 pounds sugar
    1/2 gallon hot water

Wash fruit carefully in cold water. Put fruit into a stone crock and mash up well. Add the hot water (should slightly cover fruit) and 5 cups of sugar, mix well.

Place a clean piece of cheese cloth (doubled) over stone crock, tie a string around to secure. The cloth serves to keep out wine flies. Place the crock in a warm ventilated place for 7 days, untouched.

Mark calendar when to check. After the first 7 days are up strain well, throw away the pulp. Place the juice back into stone crock. Add 5 cups of sugar, stir, and replace the cloth. Allow juice to work for 7 more days.

After the second 7 days are up, remove the cloth and when it stops working (bubbling on top has ceased) strain wine and bottle. Cork lightly at first to make sure there is no pressure build up or may blow up (breaking bottles). Tighten securely and place in a cool, dark place to age. Use corn cob for a stopper or put into mason jar. (There are many variant recipes, other wines using different types of fruits are made the same way).